Oceans & Heavens

The beauty in hellos & goodbyes

Nikita Vonee

Oceans + Heavens

The beauty in hellos & goodbyes

Oceans + Heavens: The Beauty in the Hellos and Goodbyes

Copyright © 2021 by Nikita Vonee.

Requests for information should be addressed to:

Vonee Rose Publishing LLC 820 Main Street, Grandview, MO 64030

nikitavonee.com

ISBN: 978-1-7374414-1-0 (paperback)

ISBN: 978-1-7374414-2-7 (ebook)

Library of Congress Cataloging-in-Publication Data

All rights reserved. Printed in the United States of America.

No part of this publication may be used or reproduced, stored in a retrieval system, or transmitted in any form or by any means-electronic, mechanical, photocopy, recording, or any other-except for brief quotations in printed reviews, without the prior permission of the publisher.

Cover illustrations: Nikita Vonee | Editor: Olivia Shaw-Reel

First printing August 2021/ Printed in the United States of America

Acknowledgements

To my grandmother, Rose Marie Woodley: I thank you for the lessons given in the 12 short years you were present on this side of heaven and the infinite wisdom you have provided by way of my dreams ever since.

To my great aunt, Ida Mae: I appreciate you for continuing in her place and creating another sacred space in my heart as you have pushed me to "keep on living" and finally serve this purpose of mine. I thank you.

To my parents: may this be another return for the support of my creative gifts throughout my life. I appreciate you both deeply. To my sister, Ebony: I wish we had experienced each other longer; I pray you are resting well. To my sisters: thank you both for being my first friends. To my children: you are my greatest gifts; there are no words that can express how you all have given me the strength to keep evolving to be the best version of myself. My prayer is that you learn from my missteps instead of repeating any of them. But even if you do, I'll be there to help you along the way.

To my closest friends and family: thank you for holding me up when I could hardly stand. Your support is invaluable.

Lastly, and most importantly, to my creator: I thank you for creating me to create, and spirit for developing me through the many lessons to get here to this place. It is well.

To the many women that read this book with whom I've met and those that I have yet to: I could no longer allow the idea of perfection to smother my authenticity, because I would eventually implode from holding these stories. As I walk through them, there is hope that you too will find the reasons to see the beauty in the hellos and goodbyes and all that can happen in between when it comes to love, such as I. Many of you have loved as high as the heavens and as deeply as the oceans, too; I pray that you know you are never alone in this journey.

Introduction

Chapter 1: *love is a risk to your soul*

Chapter 2: *in my grandmother's garden*

Chapter 3: *friendship—do you really have it?*

Chapter 4: *give me the keys to my Jeep back, dude*

Chapter 5: *ride rollercoasters, not emotions*

Chapter 6: *reflections of the ocean*

Chapter 7: *motherhood...the hardest hood*

Chapter 8: *heartbreak comes in many forms*

Chapter 9: *sunsets can be beautiful, too*

Chapter 10: *healing hearts come in many forms*

Introduction

I used to look for myself in others. Sometimes I found the unhealed parts of me in them. Sometimes our inner children danced around one another until we could no longer be friends. As painfully hard as it was to let them go, I knew that if I did not—growth would be a longing that I'd never attain.

I have found with each letting go of hearts, that I've found my way back to me. I was never lost; however, maybe just a wandering hopeless romantic soul in search of a love that only I could give to myself. Eventually, reciprocity became a fleeting idea, and it became apparent that my spirit wouldn't let it rest until I let go of the grip of the fairytale. My mother was right when she often said, "You came into this world quickly; you haven't slowed down since."

I have learned many lessons, sometimes they had to present themselves multiple times, but I still got them. One of the most valuable things would be that I now know that my ultimate power lies within me, my self reflection, my intuition, my self trust, love, and appreciation. No one on this earth will respect these things more than I do, so I have to be the best teacher of these things, especially to my children. My intuition will no longer be pushed aside so that my ego leads the way. Yet I will say, if these challenges had not come to fruition, would I even be the woman I am today? I don't think so.

Writing has been my release for a long time, and although I have kept the best journal entries for myself, people tell me that they have related to my selective transparency and honesty. Now I want to share some raw personal truths with you all. Although the outcomes of these stories may not have been the endings that I'd hoped for—that doesn't mean that my pen will ever stop writing these truths. Actually, it's the reason that it continues, because there is healing there.

"Sometimes life has to shake our core so that we can no longer remain complacent. And the people that remain when it's all done are exactly where they need to be—with us. Those are the places where 'Oceans & Heavens' are created."

Chapter 1 | *love is a risk to your soul*

Dear love, I have felt the highest of the highs in your presence. It's grounding yet elevating. Serene and peaceful. It seems as though we exist only in that hidden space and time, together. Like a really good love song, I want to hear you over and over again as we talk for hours like nothing else matters, because it doesn't at that moment.

With forehead kisses and strokes of my hair as I simultaneously run fingers down the outside of your arm as we lay, I am safely wrapped in your embrace. Feeling so warm from the night before as my head rests on your chest just right, a perfect indentation created just for me. That's the reason I don't want to leave you; I'm paralyzed in bliss.

I inhale you deeply as your scent graces my nose. I am grateful to have experienced this level of love that I can recall in the moments that I feel alone; you still feel close. You remind me of the sun that hits my face ever so gently on the prettiest tropical beach, a paradise. So warm and inviting. See, I want to reside here for a while, in the heavens. To be soft and highly adored like the clouds, I feel light.

I can safely rest my troubled mind inside the net of your words. It's so beautiful to be here; that's why I keep choosing you. Although I have met you a few times, I've discovered that at times I was in love with the idea of you, without boundaries. For the sake of this heart of mine, I am choosing to value the love for myself more than only what you decide to present to me. And if those two things align, I will continue to pursue you.

I was engaged to be married by the time I was 19; I had not even finished college yet. Within a year, I dropped out of school, got married, and became a stepmother of two, while pregnant with my first child. Looking back, I have thought, "Girl, what the hell did you think you were doing?" I was not securing my future as a woman, because I was too busy trying to be someone's wife and was not ready for all of the responsibilities that came with being his. After the birth of my daughter, I entered nursing school, because being a stay-at-home mother did not suit me at all. I had pushed my dreams of becoming a recording artist to the back burner as well. I later chased that dream for another 10 years; I do regret it.

Within five years, we had three children under the age of five, and my sense of identity revolved around being a wife, mother and a nurse. I had no idea who I was outside of that. It never crossed my mind that the person that I chose to end my music dreams for wouldn't be in the same position, years later. I didn't care; I was listening to Beyonce, and I was "dangerously in love" with him, and I would do anything to stay there.

Throughout the years that I grew up in church, I was taught to love God, abstain from sex, get married, have children, and serve the church. Well, it wasn't quite that simple, but those were the highlights. I learned to always forgive and love without measure; no one told me that if you are not careful you can easily confuse unconditional love with unconditional tolerance. I found myself in plenty of situations where this rang true. I believed, "he will never do that..." and I accepted things that I later thought marriage would change. There were so many unspoken rules that I had made without knowing if he even wanted to comply with them, because our communication lacked greatly. I believe that we loved each other, but there were so many more things that needed to accompany that in order for us to sustain. We ended our marriage seven years later.

We were very young when we began dating; life happened very fast for us. That had a huge impact on the outcome of our relationship, and although I have seen countless love stories to the contrary, ours was not that. I think that unfortunately, young women in the church community have been let down in many ways, and this is one of them. At my church, the purity culture and marriage was the agenda pushed, but I did not learn the applicable skills for navigating courtship and sustaining a successful marriage. I needed more than Bible verses and women's conferences; I needed relevant life lessons when it came to the beautiful struggle of marriage. I needed more people that were willing to share their experiences out loud, forsake their ego and reputation, and provide real life significant examples of trial and triumph, instead of acting as if their closets didn't have dirty linens, too.

It would have been helpful if more married couples were honest about their struggles with addiction, financial trouble, infidelity, blending families, illness, and how they've impacted their union. I've honestly learned more about love, marriage, and divorce from strangers on the internet than couples that I know personally, because shame is an ugly beast. Interestingly, some of your favorite couples may have emotionally checked out of their marriages with their physical bodies still displaying coupledom, and you may have absolutely no idea.

I think it takes more courage to end what you know is not working, than continuing to appear as if it does—whether there are children in the midst or not—because you may do more damage holding on to what you believed things were, and I ain't talking about how it appears in these social streets. Now this is only my experience, and I do understand that it may not always be in the best interest of the woman to leave. There are plenty of studies that show that women are more emotionally and financially affected by divorce, and that's not to mention that most times they become the custodial parents to the children born in the marriage, so I get it. However, you have to be good to yourself first, before you can be to anyone else.

If you have the ability to leave a situation that affects your entire well-being, and have the right resources, considering your options may be worth it. In my most insecure moments of being a wife, I was more focused on "being married" than I was honest about the reality of the marriage itself. Now, with that being said, I have been known to jump into things quickly to fill insurmountably large voids and because frankly, it's just what I wanted to do at the time.

Although my intentions were pure, I know that I've had relationships and friendships with people merely because we were in the same place emotionally at the time. They did not last long because trauma bonds do not equate to healthy connections. Maybe these things were all a part of what I was supposed to learn on this journey. I'm thankful for the lessons. Still, I wish that some introductions didn't happen at all.

Someone once said to me in response to a blog post that I wrote, "Yes! You can't grow until you suffer." Wait, what? Why is this the narrative of most black life and love stories, much less, in the Christian relationships? *'Love suffereth long and love endureth all things'* passages, had almost taken me out, and no, I don't mean that figuratively. I believe that I, as a Christian woman, was conditioned to continue in relationships while I evolved emotionally and spiritually irrespective of if my husband did so or not.

When we were counselled by clergy, whether they were qualified or not, it seemed that absolutely nothing was off the table when it came to if we should remain married or not. Not infidelity, not emotional abuse, nor physical. Fortunately, for me, I made my own decisions and chose my best interest over the opinion of someone that has never walked in my shoes. Throughout my adult life I have carried far too many situations that were not even mine to pick up. I've dealt with emotional, financial, spiritual, karmic and those consequential repercussions, in the name of "all things love."

Initially, I did it with a helping spirit. Sometimes it was against my better judgement, and at other times, I did it begrudgingly. There were lots of things that were never my crosses to bear, but because I loved the person that brought them to me, I carried them anyway. I mistook the "united as one" ideology and our identities became enmeshed instead of complimentary. I was them and they were me, until we weren't together anymore. Religion told us, "...'til death do us part," and my soul told me, "If you don't part, death to your spirit is what you will do." And yet, I found myself at the altar again, adopting another last name and a ring to show I was worthy to have it, because marriage was the goal of love for me.

As I entered another covenant and quickly dismantled the whole thing as I picked up where I last needed healing, I remained in a self-sabotaging cycle of striving to be the perfect wife. I did this for so many years that it just became a part of who I was—"the girl with the many last names." I had to let them all go, even if it hurt, especially then, before it killed me.

Chapter 2 | *in my grandmother's garden*

My grandmother was a very feisty 4-foot-something beautiful woman. In the 12 years that I had her on this side of heaven, she taught me many things about being assertive and speaking up for myself. I'm not even sure that she realized how much I paid attention to everything that she did. I remember playing in her powder that sat atop her mirrored vanity and her perfume too, some days, while I watched her. She would hum gospel hymns as she sat and applied her favorite lotions while brushing her hair.

She was sweet, like her name, "Rose," and spicy like the hot pickles she'd give us while we were there. There was an above ground pool and a jungle gym that lined her yard outside; it would burn your hands on a very hot day if you weren't careful. Everyone came to her house for family gatherings, especially for third Sunday dinners, so at any given time you'd see the gravel lined driveway filled with cars. While school was out during the summer, my cousins and sisters, and I would visit her home and she would make us cinnamon raisin bread before we'd run errands with her.

During the times that we argued, she would make us have court in her living room; she was the judge, of course, and we'd take turns being members of the jury. It was her way of deciding who was right and teaching us to be truthful. Honestly, that's the only conflict resolution that I remember being taught as a child. I even tried it with my own children, years later, to no avail.

I think her intent overall was to model being fair, and she was an advocate for making things right. She was a member of several local organizations that helped people who were treated unjustly; she became a well-known person in the community. There is a park bench in her memoriam in our hometown, too. I often think about the lessons she taught me, and at times when I am struggling with a major life decision, I dream of her.

Sometimes I even wake up with tears in my eyes; I know that she is still with me.

I started painting about four years ago. At the time, I was dealing with depression and anxiety, and had to find a way to work through it all. Smoothing the paint over a canvas helped calm me when I was overwhelmed and being mindfully present allowed me to focus on something other than my problems. As a teenager, I would sketch occasionally, but I didn't pursue it any further than high school. Most people have known me for singing throughout the years, and a lot of my energy was given to that gift. I came from a musical family; I began to sing at the age of five in the church choir. My grandmother was an organist and most of her children were musicians, too.

I won my first talent show in 5th grade singing "The Greatest Love of All" by Whitney Houston; she was my idol and I wanted to be just like her when I grew up. I remembered being so scared while on stage that day. Looking back, I realized that I developed situational anxiety at a young age, or what most people would probably call "stage fright." I can recall being called upon for a solo selection in church and feeling nauseous immediately afterwards. Eventually, it became so bad that you wouldn't catch me on a public stage without downing a glass or two of Chardonnay beforehand.

I have done so many things musically, but I also have had a love for the arts throughout my life. I used to knock on the pantry door while attempting to find a snack, for at least 20 minutes, and you couldn't tell me that I wasn't Sheila E. But I was 12 years old when I discovered writing, and creative writing was my favorite school subject. I used to write all kinds of things, mainly short poems and plenty of longhand letters to my friends. At the time, I attended a performing arts middle school and later that summer, my grandmother passed away.

It was a sweltering hot day in Kansas City, and she packed seven of her granddaughters in her woolen fleece lined Chevy

Cavalier for a field trip; I remember the day so vividly. We argued about who would sit in the front seat, but this would be a day she wouldn't be the judge that decided who was right. Hours later, she fainted in the lobby at the local DMV and suffered a diabetic seizure. We were children, ranging from one to 12 years old; I remember we were all so confused and had no idea what was happening. The only thing that we were sure of was that we needed to call an adult. Everything seemed like we were in a slow-motion film; seconds felt like hours. I remember a nurse that also was in line attending her side and people standing all around her, frantic.

My cousin and I were the oldest of the pack, so we approached the front counter to use the telephone, and they denied us. Thankfully, someone gave us a quarter to make a phone call on the pay phone, and my cousin called her mom. My aunt worked as a caterer at the grocery store nearby, so she was there very quickly. As she ran inside in her crispy white uniform, white cake icing and panic smothered her face. By the time she arrived, the paramedics came shortly after. I stood there as she laid on the ground, feeling paralyzed and confused. That was the last we saw her alive, a memory I will never forget.

Plenty of my friends have living grandparents; each of mine were gone before I was a teenager. I often feel a bit envious if I'm honest, especially when they don't value their presence. My maternal grandmother died when my mother was 12, so I never got the opportunity to meet her. I have very limited knowledge of her, besides the short stories that my mother has shared. She and her father were close, but he passed away when I was one, and I only have a couple pictures sitting in his lap as memories.

I also do not remember much of my father's father either, possibly because he and my grandmother separated when I was young. I have, at times, looked at pictures and have imagined stories as to who they all were. I wonder what their young lives were like and what they enjoyed growing up. I believe that you can't understand where you're going until you know where you've come from, and that includes your lineage. Yes, medical history is important but what we know about the emotional lives that our ancestors led is just as important. I can only use my imagination and be curious about how both sets of my grandparents affect me to this day. So, if I'm honest, my father's mother was the only grandparent that I had a relationship with. I'm sure that's why I have such a deep love for her.

I found an old photo of myself today; it looked as though I was about two years old, and I was playing in her garden. I was so young and carefree, holding on to one of the things that probably made me happy at that age—a stuffed toy. I was surrounded by the beauty from the flowers in my grandmother's garden, where eventually I grew up and enjoyed many things. I thought about how as time went on, I had unfortunately conditioned myself to stay too long in places that were dying. I am a flower, like the ones in that picture, so how could I grow if I was planted in soil that was not properly being fed with love? Now is the time that I am returning to my grandmother's garden, albeit metaphorically, to feast from her warm wisdom of love, and continue to grow there.

Chapter 3 | *friendship—do you really have it?*

Since I was a kid, I have always had a spunky, goofy personality, and have made lots of friends wherever I go. Over time that has changed—most times after each failed romantic relationship. I would have a refractory period of about three months or so that I needed to get myself together, and even then, I'd be very selectively social. So eventually, I adopted being an introvert as a personality trait. I only allowed a minimal amount of people to get close to me and had a certain amount of people that I would refer to as my "real friends." I could count them on one hand, so far removed of who I was before. I loved the idea of new friendships, but the thought that someone else may betray me would deter me from allowing them to get close. I still have to stop myself from doing that. *Whew, child!*

Anywho, I chopped up being an introvert to requiring a lot of time to myself because "too many friends were exhausting," when in actuality, it was because trusting people's intentions had become increasingly more difficult for me. Now that I have worked through some difficult truths about my lack of discernment, I can admit that I really love meeting new people when I am at my healthiest self. And if I really like you, I will talk your ear off for hours on end. So—sorry, Drake, new friends are allowed here.

Have *you* ever had a time where you had a friend that you considered really close, but later found out that they did not feel the same about you? That's a difficult space to be in, especially when it comes to friendships that you have had for many years. I think that sometimes we feel close to people because we can relate to them with surface level things, or even temporary situations, especially when we are young. And as we progress through life and evolve, we later realize that we don't have much in common anymore. I believe the saying to be true, "people come into your life for reasons, seasons, lessons or blessings." Every person that you meet is not meant to stay connected to you forever.

I've had plenty of friends that I bonded with over gossip, drama, or maybe just working at the same place at one point. As time progressed, the friendship fizzled out because there wasn't much substance or much else to discuss. Sometimes the person I considered as a friend may have had a hard time working through life situations; it consumed their energy so much that they didn't have any left to give to our friendship. That has been me, at times, as well. I pray that all my friends heal from things that they keep hidden. It could possibly be that the place that you are in life does not resonate with them anymore, and they don't know how to express that to you. And that's okay, because people may need to separate from us too, to elevate.

There are two sides to that coin; I think that one is the toughest of the two. When it comes to friendships, usually there is not a definitive ending or even a conversation unlike romantic relationships; you just drift apart. Maybe your experience is different, but in mine, that's how it has happened. Avoidance is easier than an honest conversation sometimes. It's like ghosting in a friendship. The text messages and phone calls are far and few between, meetups happen more infrequently, if at all, and passive-aggressive behavior can happen as well.

As I became more self-aware, I have learned that, at times, when I was codependently attached to a romantic partner, I was the one being less of a friend. I have had a few friends that were understanding, and we became connected again, thankfully. And I am not saying that lightly because I have apologized to them for making them feel like they were disposable. Although that wasn't my intent, I still had to acknowledge how they were affected. Being 100% authentic and transparent about your experiences and emotions are the foundation of a good friendship.

Conversely, we must give people the space to deal with life circumstances that may not have anything to do with us, and they are not ready to discuss. It can be self-centered for you to think that because someone isn't talking to you frequently, that they have an issue with you. Sometimes people are just trying to work through their own shit, and they don't have the capacity at the time to handle outside energy. Sometimes it really could just be that they don't want to burden others with their problems, but either way, it really is sad and can be hurtful. When left unspoken, it can leave you assuming that you've done something to sever the connection.

If you feel like you don't have people close enough to you to share what really is happening with you, do you even have close friends? I have been on both sides of this fence and neither have been easy. I really thought that I was isolating myself at times because I just really had a lot of heavy emotions that I was trying to work through, and others just saw that as me being distant. Just a thought, if you ever find yourself in a place where you are unsure about your friendship, try approaching it as if you were trying to reconnect with a romantic interest. Schedule a time to sit down and have coffee or dinner without your phone, or at least have a phone conversation so that you both can discuss how you feel instead of assuming. Sometimes women are so quick to make repairs to our romantic relationships, yet we often don't extend the same grace to our friendships.

I have read more about loyalty when it comes to family members versus our friendships and giving them the same benefit of the doubt, if we still want to remain close. I can remember a time where I felt that I had finally established myself as a wife, mother, and a professional, and my tribe reflected that. However, when I later found myself as a woman raising her children independently, that changed who wanted to be around me, apparently. Being excluded from certain friend groups or communities after divorce is usually not something that people want to talk about. You may hear the excuses about last-minute planning, or it being an event for a small group of people, or even plainly "I didn't even think about it, my bad." Hardly ever is there a time that people will be honest with you and say, "Hey, you're single now and I don't think you fit in with us anymore."

I'm not writing this because I want to have any pity for me; I'm sharing because I'm sure that I'm not the only one that this has happened to. If you are a person that has done this to someone that has recently broken up with their spouse or one of your mutual friends, hopefully this will give you a different perspective and you can be more empathetic. You are *definitely* allowed to outgrow friendship circles, or even feel that people don't belong in that circle anymore. An honest conversation would be the more mature approach than acting as though the friendships never existed.

This has happened to me twice. It was almost as though I was slowly ushered to stage left and separated from the married women with children. I was later welcomed back, alongside new members, after I was coupled again. That's not true sisterhood anyhow, and although it stung a bit, honestly it was helpful. Because if I can't have total acceptance in showing up as my whole self, I don't want the connection.

I have come to understand that maybe those couples were only in my life for a season as well. I choose what was best for myself and my children in those situations, and if that makes me too different to be a part of that circle, so be it. I'm committed to going where I am welcomed. I am looking at the *hellos* that I had during the times that were exciting, and really accepting the need for a *goodbye*, even if it were unspoken. I have learned to only share certain things with certain friends, because unfortunately, if people are not ready to receive your truth, it could change the way that you think about yourself. I have been met with judgement at times that I've had uncensored conversations of my experiences. Sometimes, people are overly judgmental because they are projecting the judgment that they have for themselves. I have been guilty of this before, so I know.

I am a sensitive person; I pay attention to everything when I'm having a conversation. I watch facial expressions and body language as I speak. I even notice if someone is gazing off as I am talking. It's probably because I've become hypervigilant, or maybe I am just talking a lot. But I really just want to know that you are listening to me. At times, I hate that I do that because it really causes me to overthink, and I can get on my own nerves by doing so. Other times, it lets me know that I need to end the conversation because I am wasting my energy and breath. I never want to seem like I am overwhelming someone with my conversation or taking it over. So yes, I play close attention, and maybe that is a superpower instead of a flaw.

With each chapter in my book of life, my circle of friends has changed. Sometimes there were people who were very close, and sometimes those close people were so distant that I did not recognize them. They may have even felt the same about me too. I've only had a few close girlfriends over the years, so I have never taken a girls' trip. I used to look at my friends and envy that they had lots of girlfriends to hang out with; then I realized that I am just different. I have discovered so much about myself and others throughout these different friendships. Some of us needed each other in certain parts of our lives and some have lasted for years.

I am teaching my daughters to not push their friendships to take the backburner when they become involved with someone romantically. You need your friends, whether you're in a relationship or not. It is not healthy otherwise. My girlfriends have been some of the best supporters during my lowest points, more than anyone else if I'm honest. They don't deserve to be an afterthought because that definitely isn't fair. If I could offer advice to young women, it would be that if someone comes along and catches their eye and heart, they need to remember who was there during the times that they didn't have that.

During the times my friendships have struggled in communication, I have thought, *"What did I do to cause them to not want to talk to me?"* And I wonder if my friends have ever thought the same at some point. We should normalize having the conversation of, "Hey, are we good? Are we still friends?" The assumption that you're not can cause your mind to go to different places; it may not even be about you. I read a quote today that said, "We often hear poetry and read books and things about romance. But what about friendships? Friendships can stand the test of time and they can see you change more than any other person in the world. If you consider them to be a good friend that values friendship, when there is a misunderstanding, you should repair it."

One day, I had several social media memory posts pop up from previous years. I knew exactly what was going on in my life when I wrote, "God is so good, he won't give me more than I can bear." When, in fact, I was hanging on by a thread emotionally. But ah yes, Christian cliches seemed to always soothe the mind in denial just right. I said out loud, "Damn, girl, you were faking it back then!" My best friend said to me, "I don't think you've ever been fake; I think that you have always tried to do your best." Another person said, "Girl, you are a woman trying to figure it all out, in front of us." Both of those statements were very affirming because negative self-talk is real in these streets.

I have a couple of friends that have literally seen me in all aspects of my life, including the times when I didn't think I could move forward or times when I questioned if I was making the right choices as a mother. They encouraged me and helped me walk into the next chapter of my life, and for that, I'm grateful. There is nothing comparable to a deep-rooted friendship, no matter how much either of you have misstepped off the path. If it's real, you always come back to being who you are together because the roots are planted so deeply. That type of friend is so significant and unique that you may even have your own language, and your own inside jokes too. Good friendships with other women are so invaluable, as they are literally like the sister that you chose to have in your life, even if you already have some. They are usually the first person you want to share your biggest accomplishments and your toughest challenges with. And if they've cried with you, you have reached a special level of intimacy that's rare.

Chapter 4 | *give me the keys to my Jeep back, dude*

After my first marriage, one of the mistakes that I made was deciding to marry again so quickly, instead of dating more people. I literally had no experience. It had only been two years since we separated, my children were young, and I was sick of learning to navigate this dating thing 10 years and three babies later. I was swept off my heels by a man in the middle of my prime just after I turned 30 and began to figure out what I liked. I was partying with my girlfriends, my nursing career was booming, and I had finally broken out of my shell vocally. I began singing more publicly; I was enjoying the stage of local recognition.

Ten years after my first radio single and countless studio hours later, I was living my childhood dream as a singer. But the next thing I knew, I dropped out of my gospel singing group and halted all the local gigs, because I was more dedicated to the commitment of marriage than I was to being honest with myself that I had some more emotional work to do. I hadn't even dated him long enough to know if I actually liked him as a person before I was a Misses again by the end of that year. I remembered thinking, *"Someone wants to marry me with three children? Wow!"*

Although I had those closest to me warn that I was moving too fast, I didn't care because we were in love—or so I thought. I didn't even let any of my male loved ones size him up because no one was going to stop this Leo woman. I wished I'd had more talks with older women who were living their best divorced lives back then, maybe I would've had a different outlook and taken my time. When I finally slowed down to really take it all in, things quickly took a turn, and I came crashing down from the cloud that he put me on. I didn't know him long enough before I said, "I do," so by the time the disrespect said, "Hey, what's up?" I already had his last name.

I am a Jeep lover. As a matter of fact, I have owned three different ones over the past 10 years. The first was purchased during this marriage; I had acquired it after I had been without a car for about six months. I had totaled my previous car during an ice storm earlier that year, and at the time, he decided that I didn't need to buy a new one. His reasoning was good initially; we didn't need two car payments. Fair enough. We had only been married for about three weeks and honestly, I wasn't too good at budgeting, so this was the first decision I let him lead. I'd never been without a car longer than a few weeks since I was 18 years old, but in an attempt to put "Ms. Independent" in the backseat, I complied.

For months, I took him to work, drove his car to my job, and dropped my kids off at school and daycare. It worked, until it didn't anymore. When he lost his job a few months later, everything changed. Now *I* was the one being dropped off at work, and sometimes being left there, too. There was even a time that I had to call out of work, because he refused to take me. He became mean, hypercritical, possessive and extremely entitled. The mask had fallen off, and he had no intention in putting it back on, because I was already committed to him. I couldn't believe this was happening to me, and I definitely couldn't let everyone be proved right, so I fought through it, sometimes literally. Eventually, I was so estranged from my family and long-term friends that I was codependent and right where he wanted me.

There were times in my life that I behaved as my wounded self; I was skating through life hurting others, and accepting it, because I was hurt. It was a continuous cycle of pain that I denied I felt, and I was operating with dysfunction, while in survival mode. But even there you have to be mindful that your attempt to protect your ego, emotions and heart can cause harm. I didn't know what I didn't know, until I did. Basically, I needed to deal with my own shit. So, when the disrespect happened afterwards, I told myself that it was karma coming for me, and I accepted the inevitable abuse—verbal, physical, and emotional.

Essentially, I was beating myself up before he could get to the punch. No one should ever do that to themselves. *That* is why therapy is so important to help you understand why you do the things that you do. Interestingly, during this time, I hyped him up publicly, in an attempt to convince myself that I was making the right decision to stay with him. I thought, *"Maybe if I share the good parts of him, I'll convince myself that there is value in this relationship."* This normally happened in the "honeymoon phase" of the cycle of abuse. I should've ended things after the abuse happened the first time. He had become a different person, sometimes from day to day, and I didn't know which one I'd be greeted with when I opened the front door.

I developed anxiety so badly that my heart would almost beat out of my chest by the time that I reached for my keys, and I was too embarrassed to tell anyone. At times, I was so lonely that I felt like I was on an island surrounded by the echo of my own voice, and no one could hear me—not even if I screamed. No one wants to believe that the man that they love would resort to violence and extreme control, much less tell anyone else that it's actually happening. It started off slow and subtle with name calling and sarcasm, and overtime he saw how much I would tolerate and continued until his fist met my face a few times.

Although the bruises disappeared, it took years for the emotional scars to heal; they ran deep. It was abusive, isolating, and short lived, thankfully. And when it was all over, I moved far away from my hometown. He didn't even want me to give his last name back. The next year, I began writing poetry to express myself and eventually, I shared my writing outside of my tightly bound journals and put them into a blog. Over the next seven years, I gained more confidence and in conjunction with therapy, I began to write more candidly and became more vulnerable.

I've written songs, vlogs, and a podcast about my life experiences; I even started an art business, too. I gained a social following mixed with genuine supporters, nosey folk, and people that expressed how I gave them hope to love again. Regardless of the reasoning, people were definitely paying attention. Albeit all the things were selectively transparent of my experiences, but the purpose was still being fulfilled simply because I was unafraid to use my voice. I love that I have a space for my creative expression, but sometimes I just wish that God perfected these talents without there having to be a broken heart trail as to the reason. These things have all been healing to myself and others, but I'd be lying if I didn't say that at times, I found myself saying, "Damn, God, is you finished or is you done?" 'Cause your girl is tired.

In the beginning of me doing therapy consistently, I remember my therapist telling me to make a mindfulness journal. I believe it is a tool that therapist's use to reroute your thinking to be more mindful and grateful instead of dwelling over the things that you cannot change. I'd try this for a little while and it temporarily made me happy. At the time, I was on antidepressants and writing in a journal, too. But I really needed to get to the root cause of why my trauma was so complex. I found it more helpful to write my thoughts out by journaling and blogging when I was depressed and then painting when I was anxious.

These things, in combination with talk therapy, were more helpful than me attempting to make myself think happy thoughts and write them in a space that I could come back and read. Because that felt forced; *this* was more organic. Sometimes I would feel invalidated with my feelings when I chose to share certain things with the few people that I trusted. So, I wrote instead. I developed a great relationship with myself and started to trust myself more as well. When I did that, I was able to make hard, yet necessary decisions; I have discovered that some will not always be comfortable.

Chapter 5 | *ride rollercoasters, not emotions*

Relationships won't always be a smooth sail, but for some reason, I thought that tidal waves were supposed to happen more frequently than they should have. As a result, I ended up in the deepest of oceans, alone. I don't think any form of a relationship should be so sporadically rocky that it causes your emotions to be all over the place. If it continues to happen over a long period of time, you will begin to normalize it. If you don't understand this, by the time you enter into another, you will continue in that pattern and then it's almost like you're in a relationship with the same person over and over again.

I used to be such a black and white thinker, but now I understand that there are many gray areas in life. Most times the way that people react is likely just a reflection of how they feel about themselves, because they are projecting their inner world. Or maybe it's how they were conditioned to hold space for their own feelings, or not. Sometimes the container in which they were stored was damaged and the way they spill out personally has nothing to do with you. And because they don't know how to pour them out gently, sometimes they just splatter in your presence.

People always tell on themselves. If you listen closely enough and are intentional with understanding what the person is saying, they will always tell you exactly who they are. Sometimes we get caught up in a version of a person that we've created in our minds, and we may not give them the space to be any different when they do things that don't align with that. When their behavior shows one thing, but what comes out of their mouth is a totally different thing, we need to actually believe the action versus what we are hearing because basically, some people lie.

They lie so well that they may already have a response to things that they've anticipated you would say. It's almost as though they planned it because they knew you would eventually find out the truth; therefore, they create a story line ahead of time. *That* is manipulation, and if people choose to lie about the smallest things, why would I believe that things that could affect their relationship and connection with me would be exempt? I am learning to believe all of what I see and if I don't know the person well enough, maybe only a fourth of what I am hearing them say to me. By the time I actually witness their poor behavior, I may dishonor myself by staying connected to them because they've misrepresented themselves, or I moved too quickly and was unwilling to accept the truth. If you do this, even on one occasion, they will learn that you are easily manipulated and that you will still allow them access to you.

Until they can prove themselves true, I am no longer putting too much stock into someone I've just met. Most times when people are untrustworthy, it will show up in many of their relationships across-the-board. You will see it in the way that they handle business, how they relate to their families, and how they present themselves on social platforms. How can I expect them to be honest with me if they cannot be honest with themselves? And if my feelings are hurt in the process, why would I expect that they would take any responsibility?

Relationships are mirrors, and if someone is rarely self-reflective, they will likely have a lot of interpersonal conflict. A person who lacks self-awareness in any situation is not a person that I want to be connected with. Sometimes people have no business being romantically involved with anyone because they need to heal, myself included at times. I have made peace with situations that I allowed to happen and how they affected others. Until I was able to do that, I walked around blaming everyone else for things that occurred.

Now, at times, situations may have truly been caused by someone else's actions, but I also had to accept the accountability of staying after I saw their true character. This was a key factor in the decision to leave relationships that were no longer good for me. I am adamant to not give credit to my trauma for making me a better person, but it has helped me overcome adversity in subsequent circumstances.

At times, I mistook volatile words and chaos for passion. Because I thought, *"At least he loves me so much that we are still arguing to stay together."* Right? No. That is not love at all; it's codependency running the game. My nervous system barely had time to reset before we were arguing again; I was constantly in between fight or flight responses. I didn't even see this in my childhood, so where did this way of thinking come from? But neither did I see how to properly resolve conflict.

So, I just figured it out and consequently, breakups to making up became the never-ending musical score to these here "love stories." Emotional disconnects that later reconnected between the sheets laced with sweet whispers of false apologies, not through the true changing of hearts. A repeated cyclical travesty. The fault in my contribution, I definitely acknowledge greatly, so please don't come for me here. Of course, it wasn't "all bad." We had some great times, but the toxic situations heavily outweighed the good. At times, I covered it well, so people never knew anything, until the relationship was over.

Self-sabotage was the name of that chapter in my life that I wasn't quite ready to read aloud. When I was ready to be honest, not many wanted to believe my truth or even cared to, for that matter. The storyline I had created was much more enjoyable to think of, even if it were a half depiction of the truth. But transparency and truth has never depended on the validation of others, and authenticity goes a long way. If I needed to be the villain that gave up, so be it. I didn't care. The truth stands alone, and I stood on that; I finally accepted it, too. I also told myself there is no shame in choosing yourself, and that was more important to me than staying married, because no one would value my peace more than I did, especially those that had no consequence from the advice they offered me.

I have read that you attract what and who you are. This made me feel sad, as if I was inherently a "bad person." Then I realized an opposing view. Sometimes you are what people need, and you have the choice to oblige them or not. And yeah, that's exactly it, simply stated. I used to believe that "most people are good-natured and if they loved me, they would never betray me." It was my fault in being so trusting of a person I barely even knew. Even if I had come to know them for a while, I was still simultaneously betraying the one I have known my entire life—me. What hard lessons in Christian naivety I have learned.

Everyone is not honest, and everyone does not deserve the type of love I have learned to give. Forgive, forget, and do not place in contempt. Wash, rinse, and repeat...and you have the recipe for resentment. I have decided that forgiveness is not required for things that are unforgivable. Because honestly, some things you will never forget, and some you shouldn't. Pressuring myself to believe that I needed to, in order to move forward, kept me in bondage for too long. Shame made a home in places it should not have ever been allowed and because I'm not too fond of letting it thrive here, I let it go. And since I am being truthful, there were times I wasn't the only one betrayed; I had to be let go of by people as well.

The social media highlight reel is like a rollercoaster. You'll have fun on the ride, but when it's over, it's time to get off. It will have you out here pretending for folks that don't even really know you, or even care for that matter. And once you're in too deep, it can be hard to get out. But even if it takes you one day at a time, you must do it. Regardless of what you've shared prior, when emotional abuse, disrespect, secrets, and shame enter the building, it's time to make an exit. Those things will literally kill you, and then people will come to your funeral and say, "But she was so happy!"

I have learned that sometimes when things break, the pieces shatter so greatly, that the best thing you can do is let them remain right where they are—apart. I hope, at this point in my life, people that see me from afar on social platforms, or by reading this book, take some nuggets and learn from these mistakes. This is especially true for my children, because they are my greatest gifts and I want to teach them that their failures do *not* define them.

Chapter 6 | *reflections of the ocean*

I remembered hearing things like, "Get quiet so that you can hear God's voice speak." Although I do agree, I will also say, be quiet so that you can hear your own. My favorite saying is, "God be knowing," but you be knowin', too. I used to take it as a compliment when a man would tell me that I was the best thing that has ever happened to him, but now I realize that's not a compliment at all. It is actually pretty scary. If I am the person that has affected someone so greatly that they have changed their behavior just for me, it makes me feel like it is based on a temporary condition, instead of true personal growth.

Yes, I cannot expect someone to be perfect, but integrity has to be there before we say hello. I don't want the task of making someone "better." That's too much pressure. If I'm the only reason that makes you do things in a different way, what happens when I decide that what you're doing is not enough to sustain your part in our relationship? Do you revert back? And if I leave the relationship, will you be left to your own demise? When I've done that before, I felt really guilty, and I don't want that responsibility. I'd rather be like ships passing in the night than to be your one and only anchor. Because that shit gets too heavy.

I often wonder, *"Why do I think that because I was raised a certain way that everyone else was as well?"* That's not to judge them, because everyone has their own path. But sometimes, although I knew this logically, the reality of it didn't occur to me until it was too late, and I was knee-deep in situations where I didn't belong. My father taught me to be very honest, and at times when I didn't listen to that, I regretted it. I assumed that the people that I chose to be in a relationship with would do the same, especially if they were a Christian as well. But that's not true either. It took a while for me to discover that some people are raised to survive, and subsequently raised themselves.

The truth in that is saddening. I didn't have the capacity to give what their caregivers didn't, but I definitely tried. Now it's almost as though I've reached the highest level of a Super Mario Brothers game, like when I was 10 years old. I feel so confident in my inner spirit that I know that if this type of person approaches me again, I will see them from far away, and not entertain the idea of attempting to fix them.

The stories that I've had locked inside of me have needed to be released for a while now. For my own healing, and maybe someone else's as well. Maybe it's you, maybe it's your mother, your daughter, or even your grandmother. It could possibly a friend that hasn't even told you her deepest secrets because she's afraid that you may judge her. I'm glad that I have the courage to share now. I can remember times that I wrote in my journal, and I just let my tears speak for me, because I couldn't find the words. No one should ever feel that misunderstood. After I learned to name the feelings that I had, I would share them with people that I considered close, and sometimes they would be overwhelmed by my emotion.

So, I developed unhealthy ways to cope; I had to get rid of them to detox myself from the things that attracted the wrong people. When I felt invalidated, I'd post a selfie online to get some attention, I'd reach out to people that I should have left in the past, and I'd even turn on some sad songs just to make myself cry. I knew that God gave us tear ducts to release the pressure and endorphins, but when I would sit for hours and do this, I knew that I needed to change the situations that were actually in my control.

I can remember times when I was so wound up and as I attempted to write, the only thing that happened were my pages being soaked as the tears hit the edge of my pen. They spoke more loudly than any words I could've mustered up. To me, to God, and to my spirit. I had gotten to the point that I hardly trusted anyone to tell these truths to, besides my therapist. Imagine entrusting someone so close several times over and to have them betray that. Who could I truly trust if the person that I thought God gave to me tried to destroy my self-esteem? Of course, those emotional walls went right back up quickly. Every time that I chose to deconstruct them, one at a time, another blow came and completely shattered everything that I thought I had rebuilt.

As I began to uncover where the healing was needed, I learned that, in order to have a healthy friendship or relationship, I had to be vulnerable again and eventually let some light in between those walls. I had to let people see the spaces that I covered up for so long that I forgot existed; I had to make sure that they were worthy to see them first. Sometimes we can be so hard on ourselves, and people aren't even thinking about the things that we play like a reel in our minds. They may be more interested in knowing how you were able to overcome those things versus talking about why you were even there in the first place.

So, I will say to you: *let those old narratives go.* You deserve people to know your stories and to uphold you even during the times when you are continuing to walk them through. You deserve grace and compassion in that space, too. I have learned that the most vulnerable moments that I've had with the people that are closest to me, were times when I was really 100% authentic. Even to the point where I had to say, "I don't want to hear your advice right now. I just want you to hear me." Nothing else helped me at that moment. I have said it to my parents, family members, and friends too. I've even had people say to me, "If I were you, I wouldn't have put that on social media." But look where it's brought me. Look at all the women's lives that are going to be impacted by my willingness to let them know that I have struggled too, and they are not alone.

I have created businesses through my adversities; I've had speaking engagements; I've won awards for sharing my truth online, and here I am writing this book. I'm not even fully who I want to be, yet I have so much more growth. I am working diligently to meet the next version of myself. So don't let anyone talk you out of the things that God told you that He would do... not even yourself.

About 11 years ago, I had a pastor say that one day I would speak to women, and that one day, my stories would impact them greatly. I literally pulled away from her and shook my head, because at the time I was in the midst of a terrible situation, and I thought that I'd never be worthy. I almost let the fear of judgment make me miss my purpose. My words are healing, and I am a healer too. I had to accept that. If I can help people during their darkest moments, I know that I am fulfilling this call.

There have been so many times that I've had to balance faith, fear, healing, and perseverance simultaneously. At times, it's been so consuming that I wonder how I've gotten this far without wanting to take my own life. I've heard people say that their children have kept them thriving; I know that feeling. I had to get to the point where I searched these stories and scrubbed the bottom of the oceans in my life so that I didn't end up back there again. When I had most of my "valley moments," I was 800 miles away from my core support system living in a new state with my children.

I had many days where I just sat and cried, wrote in my journal, and prayed while they were in school. The only comfort I had were the songs that I repeatedly played, hoping that they would help me to understand where I was. I'd say, "God, how did you let me get here? Why did you feel that I can bear the brunt of such a huge task?" I needed those experiences so that I could grow and present them to you now. So, at least it was not all in vain.

As a woman going through hard times, you need a sounding board, and a reservoir to hold space for the emotions that feel overwhelming. You don't need a tennis court to spar verbally back-and-forth with you just to show you that they care because they're willing to engage in the sport of screaming and arguing. That's immature behavior. When I had new connections with people, initially, I would hold back in the beginning because I was afraid that what I was sharing was too much and it would run them away. I don't go full speed ahead with friendships or relationships now; I just pace myself.

After you've begun to do the emotional work, time and intuition will reveal anyone that is willing to run away because their emotions cannot handle yours. And if so, they are not deserving to be close to you anyhow. Let them leave. If they were holding back what they had gone through in an attempt to show you that they weren't harmed by things that greatly affected their life, they aren't in touch with their emotions anyway.

When I thought that this was a good measure of love, I attracted people that felt the same way. Subconsciously, I thought the relationship lacked passion if we didn't argue, and I thought that I was unworthy of a person who didn't. Eventually, I knew that I deserved better, and I also had to be better as a partner by not indulging in trivial things. I started to read books and articles on healthy relationships, listen to podcasts, and continue in therapy. I had to unlearn everything that I thought I knew about how I loved and wanted to be shown it.

When you give energy to situations that are not peaceful, you disrupt the homeostasis in your mind and spirit. And trust me, you may eventually get back to a place where things are calm all the way around, but it will take a long time. Thankfully, for me, I realized that the longer that I stayed in situations that I had outgrown, the longer it would take for me to heal from them. My tolerance became very short when people showed me that they did not value my peace, as if I had an expiration date in my mind after the very first time that I felt disrespected, rightfully so. After you've endured so many times of being gaslit and belittled by multiple people, you get to the point where you say, "I'm not doing that shit anymore."

I have shared things publicly when I've felt exuberantly happy, that's true. But those are snapshots in time. Who's going to get on these free apps and tell the real entire truth? I've learned that some lessons are just for me, and I don't have to share every revelation. I've even gotten to the point in the last few years that if something jumps into my spirit, I don't jump to Facebook to share like I used to. I literally look up as I say, "Spirit, thank You. Thank You, God."

There have also been times in my life where I've had to remain quiet as I watched everything go to hell in a handbasket, publicly. I may have discussed it privately, but I did not respond publicly. Silence is golden. Although it has not always been easy, my character isn't messy. And the last thing that I want to do is give people a show. I'll let their character be highlighted on its own.

I've had men literally tell me that they have issues with their mother, and I've even watched a couple disrespect them. But for the ones that did not actually verbalize this, I saw it in their behavior. It was like I was a bystander around the corner of a building, watching a heated conversation, only to believe that it was about the person they were projecting on to, instead of an internal conflict. You would think that would be enough for me to take off and run the opposite way, but for some reason, my motherly instincts wanted to rescue them. I wanted to help them so much until they burned me too.

Still, I thought I could help them through it, not realizing the level of disrespect that was headed my way as well. I saw the little boy deep down that was hurting just like when I looked at my own son, and I wanted to rescue them. Then I had to realize that I was not their mother; I was taking on a huge task that was not mine to step into. At this point in my life, I have no desire to do that, and I won't take on a job that should have been completed before they even knew my name. Maybe I could've saved myself a lot of heartache if I'd learned that earlier, but this is not a place for shaming, so I won't do that. If anything, I have learned lessons that I can teach my son, and that have also helped me with my interactions with him so that the work will be done long before he enters a serious relationship. He is 16 as I am writing this book, and just yesterday, we had a conversation about dating.

A man approached me while we were out running errands. I immediately knew that he was interested in me, but when I turned down his advances, he actually tried to deny it. It was a really funny situation because my son and I saw right through it. After we returned to the car, it sparked a great conversation. As he is approaching dating, as his mother, it was really cool to discuss how it would look for him in the future. I am very intentional about not raising a "mama's boy." I am raising a young man that is self-aware and will have an equal amount of emotional intelligence and capacity to be a supportive partner.

There must be lots of intention when it comes to parenting. I am not one to give a gender bias and say that mothers have all of the emotional responsibility when it comes to raising sons, and thankfully, it's not the case in my situation. But mothers do have the responsibility of not coddling their sons to think that the world revolves around them, and that they can get away with many things and lack accountability. I understand that my role as my son's mother is to model the woman that he should want to spend a lengthy amount of time with eventually. My role is also to teach him that there are consequences when his behavior is unacceptable, which may even include losing the person that he loves very much.

I do not intend to deter my children from marriage because mine were not successful. However, if my daughters find themselves in my position, I hope that they will have learned to be self-sufficient and eventually know how to accept help from an equal partner, too.

I am also teaching them that potential is not enough to sustain a relationship. Even if you have love, there still has be an equal understanding that each partner must do self-work, because otherwise you are headed for failure. They can do whatever they want to do in life; I just hope that they remember the things that I taught them and may those things help them become successful.

They must be willing to meet me in a place of peace, after they've met theirs, because that's what reciprocity in a relationship looks like in my eyes. Fortunately, the lessons that I have learned have shaped me in a healthy way, instead of causing bitterness. Now I am using the oceans as reflections to move forward.

Chapter 7 | *motherhood...the hardest hood*

I have always wanted to be a mother, and each of my children were created with intention. My oldest daughter was born right after I turned 21; I walked down the aisle pregnant with her. I began nursing school shortly after she was born, because I wanted to have a career that was sustainable, and honestly, we were broke. My son was born two years later—his dad's namesake. I had only been a nurse for six months. I took four weeks of maternity leave and started right back working the night shift.

By the time my youngest was born, I had returned to college again for a second degree. I was attending school during the evenings and weekends, and managed to still work overnight shifts at the hospital. Needless to say, their dad was responsible for a lot of their care while they were young. He'd had plenty of experience with his older two children, so it was all good.

After our divorce, we struggled in navigating co-parenting our children. We had been together for 10 years by that time, and we had to figure out how to still raise children together, but separately. I wish I'd read some books and talked with divorced mothers to have better tools. There was so much resentment and unresolved issues between us that we couldn't see past them to work together effectively, and I'm sure our children felt the tension too. We were able to celebrate our children's birthdays together a few times, but outside of that, the conversations were minimal.

Years passed and we had gotten back together. I was willing to accept almost anything when it came to him because I loved him so much. But I will also say that the toxic #relationshipgoals social media culture will tell you it's "true love" because you all have reconnected, even if the idea of giving the childhood I had to my children was the driving force. No matter what I overlooked to attempt to get there and no matter how many mountains I climbed and conquered—I realized that sometimes it just doesn't work like that.

When we remarried, I took on the responsibility of mothering a child that was created while we were divorced. I found out weeks before my children and I were set to move back home. Initially, I was shocked. I had an instant family at 17 years old, with him having two children prior to our relationship. Honestly, I was looking forward to finally being a family with only our children in our home. But I wanted our family back together, so I took it in stride and said, "We will figure it out." By the time reality hit, the baby was here, and I had to really deal with how that made me feel. I didn't even tell my family, until I had to.

I'm still not sure what I was ashamed of. I knew that I didn't want to leave the relationship at that time, but I also didn't know if I would be able to accept a child, and a newborn, no less. I decided that I needed to go to therapy because I needed someone to help me figure this out. I visited her weekly. It was the beginning of my consistent sessions six years ago.

About six months later, I sat my children down to tell them that they had a baby brother, but they were already told by his family. They were excited to meet him, and eventually, I was too. I didn't know how much I would love him until I did; I fell in love with him after seeing his big brown eyes for the first time. It was nice to have a baby in the house. I was so used to a perfectionist complex, that I publicly put on the facade that he belonged to both of us. Although I never actually said that he did, I did not tell people that he wasn't when they assumed. If you knew, you knew, and if you didn't, good.

He looked like my other children as well, and because I had just recently moved back home from out of state, it made that narrative even easier. Looking back, years later, I realize that it was unfair to his mother, even if she was unaware. But I wasn't ready to deal with what I thought this meant for our "new" relationship, publicly. I couldn't be honest with people, because I wasn't honest with myself and how it was truly affecting me. His mother and I got along well. We spoke often about him. It was as if she and I co-mothered her son, until we didn't anymore.

By the time my children's father and I decided to divorce a second time, three years later, they were back together before the divorce papers were finalized. I'd love to say that I handled that situation calmly, but I didn't. The betrayal ran deeply, and I was furious. I had created a relationship with another child that did not belong to me, and I had to face the possibility that he may not even remember my face in the years to come. I spent so much time with him that I had hundreds of pictures and videos that I'd watch for hours.

After we split up, I grieved as though I had lost a child of my own. It wasn't until a year later that I could listen to a story about him that my children shared or came across a picture without crying. The grief was heavy. That was a tough lesson to learn. To all the women that have carried children in their wombs, their hearts, their dreams, or their spirits, and for those that have loved and longed for babies that they will never meet or that they have lost, I speak healing into your hidden spaces of pain.

Our co-parenting was affected greatly by this, so eventually, it became parallel parenting. We couldn't hold a conversation at all surrounding our children, and I was often stonewalled in text messages. I had to allow my children to be the only ones to communicate with him, but not by choice. I eventually realized that I was fighting a never-ending battle trying to force anything else. Once I let go of the resentment that I held because things weren't happening as I wanted them to, it got easier. The children had to be the focus on how I related to the person that I created them with; I was tired of fighting with him.

I decided to give up what I thought co-parenting should look like, and just let it be. Parallel parenting was the most ideal situation for us for a period of time, especially after 20 years of making up and breaking up. It was effective. As my children have gotten older, we've gotten better with our communication. I had to learn how to work with him at a distance, and heal from my issues with him too, because we will always share treasures in human form together.

I have been asked, "Throughout all of this, what has been one of the hardest things for you?" I responded with, "Having to heal while still having the responsibility of being a mother each day." It has caused me to dig so deeply in these stories, that I can hardly explain what it feels like. I do joke about motherhood being hard, but that's because it is. It has forced me to think about how my decisions affect someone outside of myself greatly. I also have learned that we condition our children in many ways—not limited to conflict resolution, self-identity, self-respect and self-worth. I am committed to teaching them how to identify disrespect, how to reflect, and when to pivot when they need to.

I have this journal that I started after the divorce, and I wrote in it almost every day for close to a year. There were some days that I missed, but I was intentional to capture what I was feeling frequently. When I found myself here again with the same person, I had a game plan written in this journal for my future relationships while simultaneously over-analyzing every single decision I had made to that point. I was so hard on myself and I didn't give myself the grace to just say, "I truly loved him; I tried again."

Maybe we really were both giving the best that we could with the tools that we had at the time, but I was a totally different person than the young lady that he'd met 20 years prior. As I look back through that journal, years later, I am realizing that I had romanticized our family being "whole" again and had forgotten the reasons that we no longer were. One of my family members asked me, "What changed? Because you have loved him forever; I'm trying to understand what happened this time." And I simply stated, "I did."

There were plenty of decisions that were so hard for me to make, especially this one. My heart had to make the choice, long after my logic did. Sometimes my spirit was there telling me what to do when I didn't think I had the answers, but I told her, "Girl, be quiet because I love this man and we can work out the details later." Later on, I have felt like I was being punished for choosing myself at times, but that was just the consequence.

Still, love can be so unfair. In the times that you must be the disciplinarian while the other person gets to be the "fun parent" for the weekend, it seems that the plight of being a mother is daunting because you only have a mere 48 hours to recoup and enjoy just being a woman. I'm not saying that I regret my decision to raise them independently, but it is tough. These are things that anyone hardly talks about when it comes to separation.

Do you remember being a young girl and getting in the car with one of your parents and just riding? Things were carefree, and there were no questions because you trusted that they were going to take you somewhere that you wanted to go. Maybe a fun place, maybe your grandmother's house, maybe your favorite corner store or to have donuts on a Friday morning before school. Well, in my experience, you can't do that when it comes to love, because sometimes people will take you to places that put you in harm's way. And honestly, sometimes they may not have been fully aware, not until it was too late at least.

However, it doesn't make it any less dangerous because you were both unsuspecting. Sometimes it's naivety, and sometimes it's ignorance, but neither of them is blissful. Joyriding can be fun, until it no longer is. Eventually, I had to get out of the car on more than one occasion. In this case it was the marriage, twice removed from the same person. That doesn't mean that he is a bad person; he just wasn't the right person for me. We were hurting the whole family, and it pained me to not be honest about that. I am no longer interested in letting anyone stay idle or drive me to places that I would not ever want my daughters and their daughters to explore.

I had to be more intentional with showing them this rather than just speaking it from my mouth, even if it were with the person that I created them with. For the sake of myself, him, and our children, I had to keep the memories and release our connection. I am very determined to teach my children to focus on who they are and who they want to become first, instead of who they can be to a partner. Within the past year, our children have been able to witness us come together and put our differences aside for them.

Now, we are finally at a healthy place of co-parenting. I believe that they are happier knowing that we can still love them in the same ways, separately, and be happy with other people, too. I won't be so hard on myself or have "mom guilt," as my good friend says. I hope that if you are in this situation, you give yourself some grace too.

Chapter 8: *heartbreak comes in many forms*

I met my third husband shortly after I had divorced from my children's father for the second time. He was handsome, charismatic, funny, and slid right into my DMs on social media. The chemistry was electric immediately following our first phone conversation, and by the time we had our first date, we may as well had started making wedding plans. We were inseparable, and interestingly, I was down for another relationship.

Over the next few months, we became wrapped quickly, and our worlds revolved around one another. He quickly swept me off my feet with gifts, trips, time and attention. It happened so fast, that this time I actually told a friend, "This feels like it's all happening too quickly, and it feels familiar." Although I knew the relationship was going at lightning speed, I wasn't afraid of storms, obviously.

Being love bombed by a romantic partner in the beginning of a relationship is something that needs to be discussed more openly. So here we are. After you have been deprived of true affection and attention for a good length of time, you are more likely to fall prey to this unsuspecting manipulative approach. You can be a highly intelligent, educated, successful career woman with sharp logic, have your finances together—and still be taken in.

For a moment, imagine being communicated with incessantly during your workday, and thinking, *"Someone is thinking of me that much?"* At first glance, it seems adoring and flattering to be communicated with so often. But in reality, it is to slow your attempt of discovering who they truly are, so there isn't much down time to do so. I remember times when only a few breaths were taken between texts of *"I think I'm in love,"* within one week of knowing my favorite color, or *"You're the most beautiful person I've ever met."* There was constant adoration, attention and flattery, and I was suffocating in the most wonderful way. I was failing to do even the most minuscule daily tasks, because the compliments felt much better than cleaning the kitchen.

We were engaged eight months later and planned for a destination wedding the following summer, but he was diagnosed with cancer no sooner than we took our engagement photos. We were both devastated initially, but I put on my nurse's hat figuratively and got ready for the ride. About six weeks after we were married, he began treatment. I spent countless hours at doctor's offices, procedures, and chemotherapy sessions, and most times, I was the only support person present.

I was familiar with a lot of medications, but not chemo. I read everything that I could and asked my nursing friends for their input, too. It was very hard watching him go through the treatments. I did everything to make him feel supported, but interestingly, we started arguing more often. I thought that it was only related to the stress of his condition, my therapist agreed, but eventually I became consumed by his very vocal unappreciation.

By spring, we were right in the middle of a pandemic, and both of us had to close our businesses down for a bit. Thankfully, my income as a nurse covered our living expenses until we were able to re-open. We were at the finish line with his treatment and I was excited about having some stressors out of the way. The totality of it all had affected our new marriage greatly. But just as I was planning a surprise celebration for the last chemotherapy session, I learned that he had been unfaithful to me the previous year. It didn't matter that we were not married at the time, it was proof to me that he'd be capable of it again during our commitment.

Still, we celebrated, weeks later, with family and friends driving past our home and honking their horns in excitement, because I had faith that things would get better. But nothing was the same after I learned of this breach of trust and things began to worsen between us. We entered marital counseling that summer, but it was short lived and honestly not helpful at all. I wanted this to work so badly, that I convinced myself that things weren't as bad as they seemed. There were glimpses of hope that we could work through this, but that stemmed from me denying the reality of the truth.

I wrote some things last year during a time when I was struggling between hope and impending doom. I quickly went from writing blogs about my then husband's cancer journey, to sitting for hours typing my tears out in the only space that felt safe enough to share...my phone.

There were so many unspoken words that I had for him, but I didn't share because I knew they would only be met with deflection instead of understanding. I thought this was "thee relationship" that would make up for every one that had failed before and because I put such an expectation on that, I broke my own heart. I placed the keys to my overall happiness in someone else's pocket, and the driving force was based on someone else giving me something that could easily be taken away. Needless to say, it turned out to be the biggest disappointment of my life.

A few months later, we celebrated a delayed honeymoon, my birthday, and him ending his cancer journey. It was an amazing trip with plenty of sightseeing, until my actual birthday. What should have been one of the most beautiful days turned out to be my worst nightmare. We argued and I cried all day long. I spent the entire day driving around Mexico alone, as our itinerary had become "mine only."

By the evening, I put on my fancy dress and attempted to cover my puffy tear-filled eyes with makeup and we headed to the restaurant I'd made reservations for. During dinner, he continued speaking his grievances about *me* and our relationship, before my first glass of wine arrived at the table. As I listened to him, I slowly sipped and sipped some more, until eventually the entire bottle was gone. At that time, I said, "If you want a divorce, you can have it. I can't do this anymore." He looked at me in astonishment.

Moments later, the waiter brought my hand-crafted birthday dessert and he asked for my phone to take a picture. As I held the sparklers in one hand, I didn't even have the energy to fake a half smile that I knew would be plastered on social media as he said, "Happy Birthday to my beautiful wife!" We quickly left, and shortly after I said, "I'll have my lawyer draw up papers as soon as we get back home." I then saw the rage in his eyes as he removed my seatbelt and opened the passenger car door, as he drove and said, "If you want to divorce me, you can just get the fuck out now and leave. I don't care if one of these Mexican niggas rape you." I quietly stared at him, as I thought of my safety at that moment.

I slowly put my seatbelt back on and closed the door. There was radio silence the rest of the way to the hotel. It was dark; I was afraid, humiliated, and traumatized. After arriving, I attempted to sleep as he continued to tell me how I pushed him to say such volatile words to me that he had no self-control because of it. I was so upset that I was visibly shaking, and I didn't sleep a wink. Eventually, I said all the things that I had suppressed throughout our 19-month relationship. I was not nice; it was freeing. Out of all the statements I said, I will never forget this one, "I am a flower, I need to be handled delicately; you don't deserve me." He replied, "You're right, and I deserve everything you're saying."

Still, the damage was done, and so was I. I did not deserve to be hit with bullets from the war that he had within himself; this wasn't my battle. I got out of the bed, turned on some soothing music and sat outside our room on the deck for several hours as I spoke to my grandmother in spirit, searching for clarity. I never felt tired; I'm sure it was her way of protecting me because there was no way that I'd be able to sleep comfortably after that disrespect and not to mention my adrenaline pumping.

I tapped my foot to release the negative energy for hours as I listened to the crash of the waves and Sade's singing in the late night. By the time that the sun rose, there was a calming peace that came over me and I felt lighter. I moved closer to the ocean and sat in a cabana as I prepared myself to pack my things and return home later that day. Shortly after, as he checked out of the hotel, I looked at my social media and was greeted with a post wishing me a Happy Birthday, a day late. *"I want to wish my beautiful wife a Happy Birthday. You're a flower...sometimes I don't deserve you."* Those were the words that I had said to him the night before, albeit mixed up a bit, but he was definitely mirroring me.

On the drive to the airport, we had a long conversation about all that had happened. It was easy for me to accept the apology after the love bombing and public display of affection. Love bombing conditions a person to chase after the euphoric "high" months or even years after the overabundance of attention stops. And trust me, it will stop. You will feel it in more ways than one, too. Initially, slight criticism will replace praise, coupled with minimal intermittent validation, and eventually heavier weighted overt verbal slayings follow the silent treatment.

You can easily get trapped in the cycle of wanting to "get back to how we used to be." It was a cycle that he knew all too well with me and I fell for it. By the time we made it home, it was all good. About a week later, I was home alone for the first time in a while. The kids were at school, he was working, and I had time to really think about what occurred in Mexico. When he called me midday, I told him that I still was unsure of our future and that I was really hurt by his actions. He responded, "I was calling home to talk to my wife, and you just messed up my entire day!" That was classic gaslighting to the tenth power with some added blame shifting, too. But remember what I said about people that lack self-awareness? They can't see themselves, so they most definitely cannot see you either.

He later asked if he could make my birthday up to me as if that would cover for the amount of unbelievable disrespect. I declined and took a solo trip that weekend in an attempt to help me figure things out. Days later, before I even left for my trip, we reconciled. Initially, I wanted time alone to clear my mind, but we spoke on the phone every day that I was there. It wasn't until months later that I realized that he was manipulating me, even then. After I returned home, he agreed to enter therapy for his anger management but the consistency lacked after two sessions. The arguments increased, threats ensued, and six weeks later, our relationship ended in the most explosive way. We hadn't even celebrated our first-year anniversary.

I blamed myself for several months after because, again, I had ignored my intuition and my ancestors that told me to leave. But apparently, I wasn't going to be able to, until I accepted that this was no longer what I could tolerate. Over the next several months, I had to deal with the public humiliation of our marriage unfolding because he sought attention from anyone that would listen. Half-truths were being shared, and I'm not sure that he could keep up with all of the different versions he told others.

This went on until the divorce was finalized, and I hardly said anything in response. I had people reaching out to me that I had never met, and some that I knew, pleading his case for him because he was blocked in every form of communication there was. There was a protection order in place, but it didn't stop him at all. He sent gifts to my home and business, called my business line, and even emailed love songs all in an attempt to "win me back." This continued until weeks before our divorce was finalized six months later. By this time, I had emotionally disconnected and had gone back into consistent therapy sessions; I was impenetrable. So yes, I didn't "fight for my marriage" during this time, because I had been fighting him throughout it; this was the coup de gras of all acts and I was done.

He learned my deepest, darkest secrets and hidden desires; I had a habit of sharing things too quickly with people that I barely even knew, because I lacked discernment, and because I am so honest. I was giving away the keys to my insecurities and they knew exactly how to drive me to the familiar places of toxicity, because I provided the GPS. Insanity is doing the same thing over and over and expecting different results, and that's exactly what I was doing. Choosing partners that may have reflected someone that I have been in a relationship with before was a deep familiarity, unknowingly or not. Although those faces had different smiles, their spirit was eerily uncanny. The writing was clearly on the wall, but because I couldn't be honest enough with myself to say that I needed to turn around and go the opposite direction, I didn't.

I can't blame all of that on them, of course. I definitely had the responsibility of making the choice to stay when everything in me was saying the opposite. But maybe I needed to be in that place in time to recognize that the triggers were leading me to the work I still needed to do. Although those situations have caused me deep grief, they also helped me on this journey of self-discovery, and I'm taking the lessons. I've always said that if you really truly love someone, you never stop loving them, you just learn to live without them and move on. That also goes for if you think they didn't truly love you back.

I will not change how I continue to love others based upon the inability of a few people loving me correctly; I will just be more careful. One of the most unfortunate things that happens when you trust your heart to lead the way is that you can be the person that suffers the consequences from a problem that was never yours to have. It's almost as though you are collateral damage because you chose to give someone a chance, and they've mishandled the opportunity. I have been caught between spaces where I wanted to love someone so deeply, and also knowing that they couldn't reciprocate it, because they didn't know how to.

Unfortunately, I was the one holding the shattered pieces until they cut me and I had to drop them. I have overextended my heart's capability trying to mend theirs, because I had unconditional love confused with boundless boundaries. I don't want to be anyone's ride or die chick anymore; I need to know exactly where you're taking me. I will give that title to the next woman very quickly, but honestly, she doesn't need it either because eventually her heart may go to the places that mine have seen, or even worse. That is not a badge of honor to have, and I hate that the era that I grew up in pressed the phrase so hard in the songs we bopped to on the radio.

There are too many to name, but let's just say that the combination between the fairytale princess love stories and those R&B jams created a very naïve young me. It had me believing that if you love your man so greatly and do everything that you could to help him, happiness will come, eventually and that type of "love" would always be returned to you. I've learned that this culture taught them that they could do most anything in life and even if it affected you more greatly than them—you'd still be there. That's unconditional tolerance, not synonymous with forgiveness and unconditional love.

One may say, "Well, if it were that bad, why did you stay?" Easy. It was not that bad all of the time. Abusers do not abuse all of the time. Sweet apologies whispered while laying pillow side, expensive gifts, roses after stating my disgruntlement, followed by weeks of, for lack of a better phrase, "acting right," is why I stayed. It was purposeful confusion that was masterfully calculated. There was more love bombing, even more grandiose than the initial phase of dating. That's why. Until you emotionally disconnect, you will fall prey to this cycle of abuse every time. Bombs are for war, not love.

As young girls, we are conditioned to be mothers. Even if one day we never become that, we most likely have had several baby dolls that we treated like our children. What did you do when you had a baby doll? Changed the baby, fed the baby, told it to stop crying, and in an imaginary way, you figured out what it needed. I have been known to calm the fussiest babies and often had someone else's child with me at any given time when I was younger.

I have been in romantic relationships with partners that had not been taught how to regulate themselves after having huge emotions, so as a nurturer, I attempted to figure out how to help soothe them. This was not my task to take on, but just like many other things for me, I saw it as a challenge. In my attempt to figure them out, especially if they chose the silent treatment, I enabled them instead of letting them communicate their needs to me. I wanted them to feel better, and essentially, I wanted to feel better as well. I thought, as a wife, *"I need to help him figure this out,"* assuming that I had to meet all of their emotional needs. Sometimes that meant that I accepted very immature behavior, possibly including a tantrum, until I no longer did.

Over a period of time, I had begun to read several books about emotional intelligence, codependency, attachment issues and narcissistic abuse. I quickly realized, this is not partnership, it's parenting. Nothing will turn you off more quickly than being expected to fulfill sexual needs after having to function as a parent to your spouse. The lack of self-awareness and entitlement are insufferable and exhausting.

As I became more self-aware and emotionally healthier over time it was as if a light bulb came on and couldn't be turned off. I was healing some deep ass wounds—ones that I had avoided before, because they were too painful to admit that I had them. Yes, people were attracted to my light, but I was quicker to recognize if their intentions were pure or not. I nipped unacceptable behavior in the bud quicker; I stood up for myself easier, I kept hold of my boundaries, and I told people to leave. I controlled what I accepted, and someone's bare minimum self-awareness was too high of a price for my soul's work. A willingness to enter therapy only after our relationship was in dismay wasn't enough for the place I'd come to. I'd say, "What do you need to work on within yourself aside from how you relate to me?"

There *had* to be a want for personal growth. I was so used to receiving whatever breadcrumbs someone offered up emotionally, that it became the norm, until it caused me ocean-deep injuries that I had to find my way back from. I had to accept this truth about myself before I could truly move into a place of peace, and believing that I didn't deserve a loving and safe relationship, platonic or romantic, was a falsehood. I wasn't broken; I was wounded. I didn't need to be fixed when I was wounded. I needed healing. Until I really dug deep, I unconsciously attracted low vibrational people because that was the reflection that I felt internally, no matter what the fair beauty in the mirror showed.

I believe that it's deeper than low self-esteem, and I wish more people understood that. When I constantly believed that I was a victim of someone else's decisions, I took away the accountability of why I accepted their behavior to begin with. And if I didn't investigate that, it was bound to happen again. It really didn't make any logical sense otherwise. After all the relationship drama that I'd had throughout my adult life, I didn't have the desire to fight about the details of this one ending. I knew what was true, and I didn't have anything to prove.

I no longer had the endurance to be in another situation that drained my energy and demolished my self-esteem, just to look back on the longevity of it and be falsely proud. If the "ups and downs" of a marriage included infidelity, abuse of any kind, disrespect, or overt unappreciation, I did not want that shit. I knew what I had tolerated before, and I wasn't doing it again.

The women of our generation are much different than those of our ancestors. And although I know that they did the best with what they had, we have more knowledge and resources now, so why would I continue to put myself through things that I did not need to? Yes, I kept choosing marriage because I wanted to, but I also chose wrong. So, if anyone thought negatively about me because I later chose to end these marriages quickly, oh well. If they truly knew all of the facets of these stories, maybe their judgment would differ, and even if not, that's fine too.

I was "struggle-loved" out. I have chosen to not live my life for people that don't have to deal with the consequences of the advice they are giving me. This is my life; it's not a democracy. I have let myself feel all the emotions that have come with this ending. In the beginning, every day was a mystery. Am I going to feel empowered today, sad by noon, or afraid before bed? I had no idea. I just let whatever wave of emotion flood over me when it decided to come, and then it passed. Slowly, I gained more peace each day because strength was not what I lacked at all. I needed to come to a place of acceptance of what was. I knew that if I didn't do that, I'd be back in the same space I had experienced before—quickly accepting the attention of someone that was not good for me.

Chapter 9 | *sunsets can be beautiful, too*

There have been plenty of times that I have small epiphanies about these stories when my mind is quiet. There are times when I remember situations, and see them in the manipulative ways in which they were meant to cause me to be confused. Sometimes I let the thoughts pass, and at other times, I dwell, for hours. I can find myself in a self-loathing rabbit hole of emotions if I am not careful, especially if I get caught up thinking about how I could have done things differently. But I cannot change the past, and thinking about how I could have definitely doesn't help me either.

My therapist taught me something that I keep in my toolbox if I find myself in this place. She said, "When you have a thought or emotion that seemingly 'comes out of nowhere,' become more curious about it than judgmental. If the thought seems to linger and is challenging, imagine there is a balloon over your head with the thought inside, and pop it, figuratively." That's helped me a great deal when I have gotten stuck in a loop of negative thinking. I believe that your spirit really knows what is true and what isn't, especially when you are in tune with your intuition. There may be times that people try to sway your decisions, because they've had a similar experience or because they don't have all the information that you do. So now I take advice through that lens and move accordingly. Just because something has happened to someone else doesn't mean that it will happen to me, or vice versa.

I also have been very careful to not take guidance from people that haven't had a favorable outcome with the same advice that they are attempting to give me. Because how does that help me? I do understand that most people are genuinely trying to be helpful, but when their suggestions come unsolicited, I feel they don't believe that I can make sound decisions for myself. And the audacity of that always runs high. I have had to learn to trust myself time and again after each heartbreak, but that's how I continue to grow and evolve. Now that's not to say that it hasn't been a challenge doing so. I have given people an easier ticket to the land of forgiveness than my own self at times.

I remember learning in Sunday Bible class to forgive people 70×7 times. I found out that when I loved them with no conditions, I had tolerated poor behavior instead of just forgiving them. I used to be ashamed to say that I have been married to three different men in my lifetime, but now I have accepted that I kept choosing commitment, because I was attempting to get it right. I just wanted to be like my parents, so much that I would rather choose marriage over dating long enough to see someone in all four seasons first.

I didn't enjoy the dating phase in my early 30s. I missed the familiarity of a family, and didn't want to keep asking someone's favorite color. After my first marriage failed, I wasn't dating to get to know someone, I was dating to replace a two-parent household. My children were young and I needed some help in my home raising them. Although their father has always been active, I wasn't too fond of the term "single mother," even if technically I wasn't one. You couldn't tell this Christian divorcee that; however, society made me feel as if I was, along with the church gossipers. But in actuality, I was just a young woman, raising her children independently from their father, and trying to find my place.

I wish I could go back and tell 28-year-old me that. Being a preacher's daughter and enduring a divorce is something no one should have to face alone. It's isolating and not to mention at times embarrassing to be asked, "Do they all have the same father?" and, "Is he in their life?" I've wanted to slap a few people for even assuming. You can live your life so publicly on the stage of these social platforms if you want to, but you will still find yourself lonely at times when you go through tough life situations. Although you may seemingly have many people rooting for you, there are very few that *actually* support you.

There have been a handful of people that have called or sent a message to check up on me, instead of using my status update as a measure of my mental wellness. Eventually, you may be excluded from your friendship circles because you are now seemingly "the weakest link" and no longer married. Sometimes it genuinely is because people just don't know what to say or maybe they have minimal interest in supporting someone that they can't relate to. Either way, it doesn't feel good at all. The invitations to social gatherings diminish along with the text messages and now you're working through real shit emotionally and cultivating new friendships, too. What a terrible plight for someone who chose to make the best decision for themselves.

I am extremely grateful for the ones that have remained and never put me in the position of uncertainty of where we stood. They know who they are.

I had an ex-partner that said he was my biggest fan. At the time, I was very flattered by the compliment but what I discovered later is that some fans don't value the true essence of who you really are. They just like what you possess. How many times have you been to a concert where there are plenty of people recording the show, only to share with the world that they have gotten close to the artist instead of really being present and enjoying the experience? There was so much work being done behind the scenes hidden from the audience, only to be unappreciated by the people they were preparing the show for. I've been guilty of this; I also have been in the artist's place as well.

But therein was the problem; I was cultivating my self-work journey to be liked by another person, instead of valuing the growth for myself. It was performative. At times that became apparent when I was disrespected by a partner and my intuition said, "Leave," yet I was holding on to the idea of who I thought he was initially.

When you value your time, energy, and space, you become very selective in who you extend it to. Sometimes it takes a few guests that overstay their welcome to get you to change the rules, and that's okay. At this point, I am no longer desiring to be in partnership with someone that sees me as a spectacle, because that's too close to being a trophy. I need someone that values where I've been, where I am, who I aspire to be, and walks with me during the process of getting there. They also must feel the same about themselves, and that they are deserving of such a partnership. After all, I am wading in the still waters of peace, and I won't let anyone disturb this groove.

After several failed marriages, I thought, *"Okay, what is wrong with me? Because apparently, I'm the common factor, right?"* And then I would tell myself things to justify my choices, right before I started the cycle of shame and rumination again. Maybe it was him? Because I was raised with two loving parents in my home; I saw a great love story in front of me. Surely, it couldn't be me. That's when I realized that two things can be simultaneously true. Yes, I had the security of both parents, and I also was not taught that everyone isn't safe to love. I was naive and lacked discernment. Still, I aspired to recreate the love displayed from my parents time and again with partners that were not capable of the task.

Honestly, my sisters and I were taught to independently provide for ourselves as young women, from parents that were interdependent. I know that wasn't their intent, but it did happen that way. That is my vantage point, and maybe theirs will differ. Now, I am also very aware that I have blind spots in my behavior and temperament too, and as a young woman, there were lots of things that time had to teach me. However, I am inclined to believe that I was conditioned to always see the best in people, even if they have at times shown me their worst. Because I was naive, I'd think, *"Is there such a thing as perfect love? Everyone has something to work on."* And simply put, it caused me to mistake huge character flaws for things that could be changed by the right woman—*me*.

I knew I could not do it alone, so there was the good ole Christian fallacy that "God can fix anyone." It got me good. I am even more inclined at this point to believe that sometimes people don't think that they need to be any different than they are, because people have tolerated who they've been thus far. Maybe they have yet to meet the crossroad of growth and complacency as I have, and that's understandable.

But that doesn't mean that my connection to them has to remain the way that it was before. I believe true change must be based on personal growth and not the fear that our connection will end if things don't change; otherwise, it will be inauthentic and short lived. I also had to come to the realization that just because I wanted something to go a certain way did not mean that it was in my best interest.

I have consequently given important titles to people that should have never even known my name, in exchange for receiving theirs. I'll admit that I met them at times more than I needed to. They were a mirror image of my soul at that time, to show me, me. Some I met many times, in different places, with different faces, at different times—yet their spirit was kindred with a familiar past love. Multiple chances I gave to these lovers, while the prancing on my heart took place, and all the while not extending the same grace to even myself from my missteps.

There is the only one regret. I took care of their needs while mine lay dormant, biding time in hopes that one day they would be noticed by my partner, too. I think the amount of love that I had for them confused me into thinking that they actually loved me the same. That was a painful realization to face. I gave up my voice in these relationships as theirs became louder, both literally and metaphorically. At times it was like a screeching violin of negative inner dialogue with a heartbreaking melody. It was a soundtrack of pain, and those critical voices pierced my spirit so deeply that even when there was a glimpse of hope, I was quickly reminded of where we really were in this "love." Depression became the result and anxiety took her place as the co-captain.

Eventually, career highlights, talent accomplishments, and creative milestones mattered less, because mastering love was the goal. Yet I was so accustomed to appearing like I had it all together, that I idealized my partners even greater when times were the toughest between us. I was attempting to prove to myself that I was capable of figuring things out, when in reality, I was doing the majority of the heavy relationship lifting and struggling to do so. By the time I succeeded in making the bullshit shimmer like diamonds, all they had to do was show up to the party and everyone thought I had it made. I was faking and failing at the same time, and I was exhausted by it all.

It wasn't always bad, but when it was, it was terrible. And some of the same tests came in similar circumstances by way of different people, multiple times. I used to think that God was the author of terrible jokes in my life, when really, my spirit was giving me a new chance at an old lesson. I didn't see it initially. I made plenty of excuses for their behavior, and subsequently the reactivity of mine as well. In the past, if someone did something to me, I believed that it reflected how they felt for and about me, every time. But what I found out was that they were behaving the best they were shown, and I was blindly following behind hoping that one of us would eventually figure it out. So, in turn, I learned with them and our hearts, our minds, our children, and even our pockets had many lessons, too.

Most people that attempt to discourage you when you make a decision that will benefit you, are usually projecting their fears. They are afraid of what their results would be if they made the same choice. So basically, it doesn't matter what type of advice people give you, *they are not you.* Live your life. There have been so many situations that have caused me to really examine my level of selflessness—as though I had blind loyalty to such a fault that I eventually became collateral damage to decisions that I had no voice in.

Although I had a changed mindset in how I'd handled some situations, I kept "hoping and praying" that things would have a different outcome. At times, I gained new information about my partners, and I still proceeded as if I didn't think it would affect me. And then I was highly disappointed when the consequences presented themselves. I could have demolished people with my truths after the ending of relationships, but I silenced myself and inadvertently let others tell my stories. I think they counted on the fact that I probably wouldn't share the details publicly, so they continued to share lies and dig up old scripts of my life—in an attempt to make themselves more believable.

Sometimes, the reactive emotions that I have had made me want to vindicate myself, but in reality, that was just my ego. So, I told her to be quiet, because "this too shall pass." What did it really matter what people thought about what I knew wasn't true? I won't lie and tell you that I wasn't upset at all, but it would be foolish to try to fight a false storyline or an old one, no less. I'm no fool.

Have you ever heard of someone referring to their partner as God's gift? Or that they are a godsend? I've heard this on several occasions in my relationships, yet I don't feel that I was treated as such at certain times. It's almost as though they received the gift that God gave them, saw it, admired it, and may have even become a fan of it before placing it on the wall like a trophy. And when they were ready to show the world or even to their partner that the trophy was valuable, that's when they pulled it out and showed the shine of it.

Sometimes it was placed back on the shelf, behind the walls and within the space that they called home. The trophy was merely an ornament—sometimes the doormat, sometimes an ATM, and sometimes even a living human space used for pleasure. I don't want to be anyone's trophy anymore because I know that I'm the prize. Being a trophy comes with many obligations that I never signed up for like being paraded around in front of exes on social platforms, or at family gatherings. And although I know that I possess beauty in the physical, I would much rather someone see my internal world as a vibrant space versus just being something to show off to others. Because, if I'm honest, they were deserving of neither anyhow.

I didn't realize that until it was too late, and when I say *too late*, I mean literally signing the divorce decree. I should not have to teach a man how to treat me. I know that we say that often and I have been one to do so as well, but men should be good humans with integrity before you even show up on the radar. Most times, however, because you may lack boundaries, they know that they can manipulate you. I have, at times, laid the story of my partner out so well, that all they had to do was show up and say, "I love this woman. She's my queen." I had done so much work on myself and was always evolving and continuing to do so that it almost looks like it spilled over into who they really were. I was an umbrella to protect them—like an awning from the sun when it was too bright, and like a safe shelter for their emotions.

But what I realized is that I was the one that was literally getting burned. Who was going to protect me in those times when rage and anger occurred because they knew they could not live up to who they proclaimed to be as my partner? That's a hard place to be in and unfortunately for me, it happened several times. I had to do some more inner work that I thought that I had already done over again, so that I could detox whatever was present in my life that made me attracted to them to begin with. They had more audacity than they had integrity. They were partners who could not even cross emotional puddles for me, yet pushed me into the deepest parts of the ocean.

I cared so deeply about them and recognized that they were in need of something that I could not give them. And even if they wanted me to be their "everything," I knew that I didn't have the capability, nor did I want that duty. I am not all-knowing; I am not God, I am not a therapist, and I absolutely do not want to be someone's everything. That's actually very unhealthy and codependent. No one should be everything to someone. You need several healthy relationships in your life to flourish, and different people to show you different things and parts of yourself. When it becomes so codependent that you lean on one person for every single thing, eventually that person gets burned out.

Thankfully, during my last relationship I did have several other outlets and friendships that I maintained during that time, because I had learned the hard way that you cannot forsake the most important people and things in life just because you feel so connected to one person in your life. So, I learned to break the cycle of codependency that I had picked up along the way of these adult life experiences. I was not going to pick them back up just so that someone could feel good about themselves either.

I do understand that being transparent selectively is helpful and smart because no one wants to tell all of their business. But when you curate this appearance that "you got over it easily," sometimes you may make people think that they are having a much harder struggle with their own breakups, and that something is wrong with them, if so. Because you weren't truly honest about how it really affected you. You're doing everyone a disservice, and you may as well keep your story. I learned that one of the things that I was doing was making dysfunction look good. I also made things that were really mountains for me look like speed bumps when I made social media posts.

I read an article that said that nurses have this affinity for people that are hurting. It's almost as though we have so much empathy for people that we don't like to see them hurt, so we not only attract people that are in this space, but we don't even realize that they may be needing something that we cannot give. We can heal them physically or help them heal physically because that is our profession, but it's like we get so used to doing that, that it crosses over into our romantic relationships.

That also has been known to be true with women that are go-getters, or bosses per se in the corporate world. We are so used to a challenge that it literally just seems as though this is something else to overcome, meaning helping someone get from point A to point B. Many of us are very successful in other areas of our lives, except for the romantic part. In one of my journal entries, I wrote that I am very confident in who I am and what I have to offer as a partner, but I have this spot in my soul for men that need help and I often confuse it for love too quickly. They were not even worthy of the love that I possess, and little did I know, I actually unlocked a new level of understanding of myself. Therefore, I'm glad that I have kept journals over the last 10 years, because you can think that you remember everything that happens but sometimes your memory fails you. When you can look back at the written words that you felt at the time, it almost places you right back in that same space. Sometimes when reading I have felt the same emotions that I was experiencing at the time that things happened.

As I've gotten older, I have learned that I love learning. I love things like personality tests, reading about emotional intelligence, and analyzing human behavior—*a.k.a.* people watching. The easiest place to find most of this is social media, and you can learn a lot about people by looking at their social media pages. Maybe I should've been a behavioral scientist or something. When I was a child, I was Chatty Cathy. Every single report card said "She talks a lot, but she does get her work done." So, I always knew that, at some point in my life, I would make a living by speaking my words. I even found a video of myself when I was about eight years old where I was very assertively telling my cousins and sisters don't come and do whatever it was that I didn't want them to do.

Being a very assertive person was not foreign to me, until I was in an emotionally abusive relationship. Sometimes I read over my journals during the times that I was really going through some heavy shit, and now, looking back, I realize that not only was I immature in my thinking but I wasn't very self-aware. It's almost like I had missed the mark to learn that these relationships were mirrors of where I was at the time. When *true* self-awareness happens, the mirror literally is in front of you, and you have the choice to accept it or to keep yourself in denial. If you continue that route, you will forever be in a never-ending cycle of finding the same people in different faces and also presenting yourself in the same way.

Now, none of this is to say that my true feelings weren't valid, but you can hurt and be hurt by something that you are doing to yourself. I just needed to be aware of it and realize how and why I got there. This came over time, however, and keeping my journals has helped. I will say that although I have come to a place of understanding of these stories, I will not minimize how I have felt while they were happening, or even afterward. Because it all matters; I didn't deserve any of this treatment. I've had to stop talking negatively to myself as well, I was not stupid, I was learning. And now that I know what I know, I will make better choices, thank God.

I have decided to look at every experience as art. Every brushstroke and every way that the art paint is blended, I wonder if I could've chosen to do it a different way. Art is art; you can't mess it up. That's what I tell my guests at my studio every single time that they make a complaint that their picture is ugly. They say things like, "Oh, it doesn't look like yours," and I tell them that's because it shouldn't. I don't say that in a mean way at all; I just tell them I have lots of practice, and your art is unique to you. Life is that way, too.

That is one of the reasons that I paint. At times when I have found myself wound up emotionally, and I may not want to externally express that by my conversation with others, I get wrapped up in expressing it with a piece of visual representation. So, it's almost like it's easier for people to take in the emotions that I have by looking at a very beautiful expression of it by way of colors on a canvas that I splattered everywhere, rather than listening to the words that are actually coming out of my mouth.

I can always "put it on a canvas" as my friend says.

I remember a time when I called a friend, who is also a visual artist, and told her how I was really having a hard time; that's what she told me to do. So, when I get to that point at any time now, that's exactly what I do, and then I feel lighter. More recently I have done the same by writing two-minute songs and then sharing them if I choose on social platforms. It was a very vulnerable thing at first, because they were the most real emotions that I was able to express using my vocal ability. I didn't want to come across as though I was sad, or even that I was having a hard time processing another divorce, but that's exactly what the hell was going on. And I had to get to the point where I just understood that people love and accept when you are honest, versus acting as though things are really not bothering you. I've had so many people tell me that they can relate because they are going through the same things, and maybe they are not ready to express it, or that they don't even know how. So as much as I have wanted to run away from the task of being people's voice, I have learned to embrace it and obviously it is helping women. I'm so thankful for my creativity.

I have often said many times that one of the hardest things that I've had to deal with is the feeling of being misunderstood. At times, in my life, I've felt like people have truly been able to see me, whether that be a friend or a romantic partner, but only later to find out that their intent was to gain things from me and not actually see who I was. And that is a very heavy thing to deal with and it also makes you want to clam up and not be as vulnerable with anyone else. But then I realized that I could share my truth with anyone, and it is up to *me* how I accept what is done with that information.

Thankfully, now that I am more discerning, I am attracting different people in my life that actually hear me and see me and truly want to know to understand me better. I can share hidden parts of myself and know that it's safe to do so. Each part of my life is like a layer and now I approach friendships and a romantic relationship in the same way. I only reveal things as far as I believe that you are revealing, and I am taking my time doing so.

One of the ways that I'm learning to no longer be a fixer of a man's problem, is if they are sharing something with me, I pause and ask, "Do you want me to give you some advice or do you want me to just listen?" I think that that question alone allows them to stop and pause and reflect on what exactly they want. I was so used to jumping in and offering my advice and wanting to fix it for them, that it became a knee-jerk response, with little thought. I was hindering them in their way of critically thinking and literally doing the work for them. So, this way works much better for me and them. It causes me to observe my own behavior and to see if I am enabling them in the moment, and it also causes them to think through the problem and be able to solve it themselves.

At this point in my life, at 40 years old, I definitely do not want to be the one making all of the decisions for the rest of my life when it comes to my partner. I need an equal, not another dependent. I had a friend say that she was rushing to marriage and not being mindful of the process, and for me that was true as well. I often find myself wanting to get to the end before I even worked through the levels of the game. Like when I was 10 years old, playing Nintendo; the Super Mario Brothers was my favorite. You had to work through the levels as the princess and slay all of the demons and jump through or over the bodies of waters onto the next building, before you got to the final level. I don't remember if I actually did get there, but the process itself was exciting to say the least.

It's almost as though I enjoyed it more because I did work through those levels, instead of someone giving me a cheat code to master it. If you pay attention to the stories of your life as a child and a young adult, they will help guide you to the next part. I have had women ask me, "How do you do it?" It may seem as though I gracefully land on my feet after every blow, but the things that they see are only the end result. With this most recent situation, I spoke a little bit more candidly during the process. I didn't tell all my business because that was not my intent, but what I have learned is that sometimes I could have been blocking someone's view of how I got through tough situations, by only showing them the end result.

I do also know that every part of my story is not for public consumption, and neither is my healing, but sometimes it could be the key that someone else needs. Sometimes people genuinely want to know; it's more than them just being nosy. So, when they have come to me with a personal message, or even a text, I have simply said the only way through is to go inside. You have to come to a place of peace with yourself—a place that is not directly connected to a person before you can move forward.

In my case, I don't let anyone decide my timeline or how quickly I decide to move on to a new relationship but me. I have learned to listen to my intuition, and to trust myself. I do not put the majority of the trust in the other person, because if I do that, I can fail. Even if that other person is not trying to maliciously harm me, they still can, because they may not know themselves as deeply as I know myself. And until you get to that point, you can continue to harm people along the way of your journey. So basically, you've got to get in touch with your emotions and the storyline of your life first.

I don't claim to know everything, but I do have a wealth of knowledge and experience when it comes to situations that have not worked out for my greater good. I read an article where the author talked about all the things that he learned post-divorce, and I'm telling you that alone helped me more than reading success stories of people that almost failed in their marriage and were redeemed by God, or something like that. I appreciated his candor, and how he talked about losing the love of his life because he did not know himself. I will always appreciate honest and transparent people versus the ones that claim that only God fixed their marriage.

I was looking at myself in pictures over the years in relationships, and I realized something about myself. I appear to be very happy, glowing actually, because I was loving the fact that I was being loved and in love. At different times in my life, I have people come to me and say, "Wow, who is this man that is putting a smile on your face? Girl, you are really glowing! Wow, I am so happy to see you happy!" But now that I am where I am, I notice that I'm happy because I *am*. I'm hella resilient. It has nothing to do with a particular person putting a smile on my face; I have just allowed things to be a chapter in my life instead of the entire story.

Now, I know that the intent behind those comments were pure, but it almost put the responsibility on to the other person that you're in a relationship with. And for me, if that were true, that means that they can take my smile with them if they choose to leave, or if I left them. One of my friends said to me that what she realized was that every time she thought that she was happily in a relationship, what she came to realize is that because those people were mirroring her, she actually was in love with herself. Now, go with me here, I believe that what she was saying was she realized that she was the person that was creating the happiness. And I agree.

It took me a while to realize that I was allowing the external validation to keep my situations afloat. When it was drowning at a time, I found myself reverting to those same things that I had always done. After a very intense disagreement or even a fight, once we reconciled and I needed to feel better and safe about the relationship, I turned to social media to put a long post up and the caption under a picture almost to say, "It's okay, guys.

We're good now." Sometimes nobody even knew that we were fighting except for me and him, but I guess I needed to have some form of assurance to let me know that it was okay for me to stay. Honestly, *that* is manipulative too.

Because I was in such a deep hole of idealizing my partner with these outward gestures of love, by the time it was over, and I was ready to be honest, it was as if I was crying wolf. I have made a vow to myself that whenever I enter a new relationship, I will be very mindful of the old habits that I have had. I will not do those things again. It reminds me of a story that I read when a woman says, "I want you to tell the world how much you love me," and the man looks at her and whispers, "I love you." She immediately said, "Well, why didn't you tell anyone else about that?" And he replies, "Because you are my world, and that's all that matters." Now, in my case, I really was trying to show people that they can have hope after failed relationships, but what I didn't realize is that I didn't even give us the chance to get to a place where we would be anybody's example. I was so focused on the outward appearance and proving that I was worthy of being "someone's something," that I didn't realize the detriment that it caused.

I didn't give us the chance to make mistakes in the relationship. I was just so intentional about saying, "Hey, look, I can do this whole relationship thing successfully." I had actually told a friend before that I never feel like I failed in relationships of the past because I knew that I had chosen me, and it was the right decision. But subconsciously, I didn't actually believe that and time and time again I have found myself making those excuses, but my behavior was showing otherwise.

I had to get "clean" just like a person addicted to a substance. Mine was falling in love. Unfortunately for me, my 12-step program included multiple marriages with heart-wrenching plots and endings, too. That's enough motivation to figure some shit out though, trust me. There have been times when I have been left with the rubbish that was collected from the things that my partner's and I have acquired collectively. But the worst part of it all is that although they may have said, "Hey, I got you," it wasn't until we ended that I realized this was the furthest from the truth.

I had to pick up the pieces of my heart while simultaneously handling huge financial commitments that we made together. I then knew that no one will have me like I have myself. So that's how I learned to become overly independent. I have been disappointed way too many times by people that said that they were my partners, when in actuality, that was very conditional. I have raised children for some, brought others back to a healthy place physically, and supported others financially, but what about me? I realized that I was constantly attaching myself to people that weren't healthy, because I wasn't either. Until I was able to change my mindset and know that nothing that they did was my fault, I kept accepting whatever they gave.

I have felt so alone and silly, at times, for allowing myself to get back into some of these places—so much so that I was ashamed to ask for help. It was almost as though I was punishing myself for decisions I made when I was literally in emotional survival mode. That's not the place that anyone should be after someone takes advantage of their kindness. To the outside person, it looked as though I was the person that was the problem, because I just kept changing partners.

However, I have never fully shared what had happened to me, until now. My heart was pure, and I just wanted to feel safe. Eventually when I got over that fear of social humiliation, I was able to truly live for myself. And keep on moving in life with love; I had to understand that I did deserve to be happy.

Because I consider myself a music aficionado and am a singer, I have figured out some creative ways to help me when I feel down. Over the years, I have created several playlists of songs that I could listen to daily. These songs helped me cope with my mood. I have a playlist that has healing songs from some of my favorite female artists, and I have a playlist that has deeply felt break up songs. I also have a worship playlist with inspirational gospel music, and then I have playlists of my favorite artists that I can just jam out to happily, more like ratchet music. I am a very eclectic person, and I like many things, including lots of different genres of music.

The art that I create helps greatly as well; I even created this book cover last summer, too. Now I know that for me this is what has helped, but maybe you can develop coping mechanisms that are positive as well. I have learned that when you go cold turkey and cut things off abruptly without ways to cope, it can affect your mental health greatly. You may even do more damage to yourself, and then you are scrambling around, trying to find ways to make yourself feel better. So, take your time and develop something that works just for you.

Going to therapy forces you to be honest with yourself; it is not a quick fix for your crisis, but more of a tool to help you cope with most life situations. When you have the right tools to navigate life circumstances, everything will not always seem like a "crisis." It will change how you view life and the things that have happened to you. You will begin to see your character flaws, possibly your own toxic behavior, and how it all plays a part in every relationship that you have. When you're ready for that to happen, that's when it will be most beneficial for your life. Otherwise, it will feel like you're just "paying someone to listen to your problems."

Chapter 10 | *healing hearts come in many forms*

Being deeply honest with myself was one of the first ways I truly started healing. I am a victor, I am a survivor, I am a goddess, and I also have hurt people, too. Accepting who I am as a whole is the only way that I will elevate to the next level in my life. Now that you have been privy to these life stories of mine, hopefully there is a greater understanding of me. But if not, at least I know that I've shared my truth and I am happy with that.

I am a creative; I will no longer silence my authentic experiences and not share how they really happened, because I'm afraid that someone's feelings may be hurt, when mine were crushed in the process. I am powerful and so is my story. One thing about being connected to a creative is that you don't get to decide how you show up in their creative outlets—so be careful in how you treat them. Because we are still going to tell our truth, whether you like it or not. Only disingenuous artistic material comes from the excessive worry about how people will receive what you are creating. People appreciate your truth more than if you appear like you have it all together. Pain has birthed some of the greatest bodies of work. Just ask your favorite artist's favorite artist. It's hard for people to relate to things if you aren't even being honest with yourself about how they happened. I want people to connect to these stories, and to know that they are not the only ones that have felt them.

There were lots of times that plenty of the same scenarios almost identically happened over and over in my life; I used to think that God had a very interesting sense of humor for my "character building." But it turns out, I had not learned the lessons yet; my spirit kept teaching me until I got it. I had to do some deep-sea diving in my spirit and change my way of thinking in order to move forward. If I would have remained stuck and kept thinking about the things that had happened, that I couldn't change, I would've never come to be who I am today. The young Nikita had to learn the hardest way, unfortunately.

In the past nine months, I've come to understand the pattern of my relationships more than ever before. Although I have never had an issue with getting into a new relationship, I realized that I was constantly attaching myself to people who weren't emotionally healthy, because I wasn't either at the time. Now, I could tell you all day that these men came from homes where their fathers dominated the women that brought them into the world; that was the reason that we failed. Albeit partially true, it had more to do with *me*.

People were always telling me who they were; I couldn't see past who I wanted them to be because I was too busy giving them the crown that they didn't quite deserve. I know that there has to be a level of trust with people when you want to be in a relationship or friendship with them, but I gave them too much credit, and often too soon. And because I also couldn't see beyond my own wounds, I helped them nurse theirs at the same time, and we were sick together. Sure, we may have both divorced the other parent of our children, or had shared past experiences, and we may have even had a few mutual friends too, but beyond that, what else was common ground? We were bonded by the traumas between us, and I was blinded by the fireworks of heavy affection on a hot summer night or the hottest tea that my mouth could stand.

Our paths had collided and what should've been a quick "what's up?" turned into a moan from beneath the sheets, and a wedding ring, or friendship that I thought would last forever. All of that drama gave intensity that I had mistaken for passion, romantically and platonically—mine from my adult love life and theirs from being children that eventually grew up to do as they saw. We each loved the thrill, and we all lacked boundaries in some way, too. I was so focused on switching up the plot for the people in the back watching me, that I was oblivious to see the real danger that lay ahead.

I created storylines in my mind about what people thought of me, when in reality, the biggest judge was my own memory. I really wanted to love; be loved and to help heal the wounds that I saw in each of them, subconsciously or not. But I was never equipped with the right tools because they had to do their own work. Although my intentions were definitely pure, I did have a habit of wanting to feel needed. So, I kept trying to repair things that were never mine to fix to begin with. Different men, different friends with different faces in the same spaces as I.

Each relationship reflected how I felt about myself at that time, including romantic and platonic relationships alike. I've had to ask myself some very hard questions after being connected to certain people in my life. So, imagine the dynamics between two people thinking that they are reciprocating their love for each other, when they are just projecting their pain. They are spoon feeding insecurities and spitting out the nutrients, day to day. It's a perfect storm for an inevitable disappointment that always ended in a massive nuclear war.

We couldn't really see each other, and we were hurting one another in the process, even if at the time we were unaware of that truth. It wasn't until I started doing my own emotional work that I realized I had no control over anyone other than myself, thinking otherwise is a foolish mindset. So basically, "if they wanted to, they would." Real love should not be that hard. Love is easy. If you want to understand your partner and grow with them, you will figure it out, together. But that doesn't mean that in the process, disrespect should be allowed in order to compromise. That would be settling for things that are beneath you. Anything that you have to force, just isn't for you. Because that's not love; it's attachment.

I came to a place of understanding so deep and realized that I was enabling these men and damaging my self-esteem in the process. I also was protecting them, even when I needed to be protected *from* them. So, I let go of each of them, one by one, and one day at a time. Having such a tight grip on these stories was wounding my hands and my heart, too. And that's not to say that these relationships were not important at all...that couldn't be further from the truth. I needed them to help me grow, but I also saw me for who I was when I was with them, and when I wasn't.

I truly desired someone who was emotionally intelligent like me, so that they could understand why projecting their emotions was futile and damaging. I needed respect, empathy, and a soft-landing place, too. I also needed someone that was willing to help me grow spiritually, emotionally, professionally, and not just be a sexual experience that says "I love you" every day. Because I know that all of these things are all encompassing what a good relationship should be about. I could no longer cherry pick and decide that one was more important than the other; otherwise, I'd always feel like something was missing.

When you become aligned with who you are and what you need, you will know when someone presents themselves with all of these things in place. You will not have to teach them what it looks like to be in a healthy relationship with you. Because if you see that they don't have all that you need for them to possess, you will eventually get to a point where it turns you off greatly and you cannot take the chance of messing up what you've built. People that have nothing to lose will help you lose everything that you have, and that includes your peace also. I am only willing to receive someone that is also willing to make sacrifices for our love too, instead of me moving mountains to get to them. They must be willing to meet me in a place of peace, after they've met theirs. Because that's what reciprocity in a relationship looks like in my eyes. Fortunately, the lessons that I have learned have shaped me in a healthy way, instead of causing bitterness, and now I am using the oceans as reflections to move forward.

A healthy sense of self keeps you from being impressed by people that can't give you what you already give to yourself. I am amazing to myself; I am kind, gentle, patient and loving too. Those are the things I expect from anyone I allow to be in my space. Otherwise, I am settling for mediocrity, and I'm not interested in hiding any parts of who I am just to be in connection with someone. Sharing who I am through the constraints of someone else's eyes is not freedom at all—it's bondage.

I recall one time that I reached out to my therapist and said, "I don't know how I should handle this. What should I do?" She simply replied, "Nikita, you know what to do. Go within and listen to self." She was right. People have often said, *"You are so strong...I admire your strength...You inspire me,"* at the very times that I was being hard on myself. Unbeknownst to them, I may have just cried for having to be those things, but God be knowin', ya know? When life rocks you, you must find a way back to being grounded and come back to center. And during the times when the waves of life have tossed my spirit so far from shore that the island of peace seemed unforeseeable, I knew that there was an anchor, even if I couldn't see it.

As I got older, I had begun to find beauty in things that were dying, like the roses that I kept weeks after they had no more life. Sometimes I didn't even realize that I was standing right in the middle of dead gardens, disguised as romantic relationships. I kept trying to feed and revive them time and again, but the soil was tainted; it was never cultivated properly to begin with. I'm glad that I now know that uprooting my physical body from these places has proven that I can flourish and pour all that I desire into myself. Because I don't have the capacity in my heart to be filled with any more empties.

After my last divorce, I had to go deep inside and reach further than I ever had before to heal this place of pain. I was discovering new wounds each day and simultaneously wrapping them with care. I saw my therapist more often; I got really honest with my support system instead of hiding my devastation. I held my boundaries in place publicly, stood up to all the people sent my way to disturb my peace, and denied his multiple attempts to win me back, even weeks before the divorce was final.

I was a warrior in my own battle, and I won this war. This level of resilience is unshakable. I have been grounded by my feet touching the ocean floor, and the only way I was swimming to the shore was by accepting help from the people that truly loved me—because I can't swim alone. Eventually, I knew I'd feel the sun beaming on my face again, giving me hope that the heavens were on the horizon. I just knew it. I have learned and I will keep moving forward. I have always said that absolutely nothing will ever close my heart to love, and I will always choose it. My discernment has gotten turned up a few notches, however.

A lot of people think that healing is this beautiful, spectacular, and joyful experience where you are elevated to levels of knowing your higher self. But if you are *really* doing the work, you drag yourself through the stories that you tried to bury in an attempt to make yourself feel better, just to retrace your steps. I had at times intellectualized my bad relationships to make sense of them, by saying things like, "He did that because of this...And it makes sense that I would do that too..." Instead of truly acknowledging that regardless of the reasoning, it still hurt me. When I denied reality and covered things, they didn't heal; they just became deeper wounds, hiding my emotions and forcing positivity did nothing but keep me stuck.

I've been to some dark places, even while recalling stories to write this book. It has also been a very healing process for me as well. It has sparked conversations with the people closest to me including my children; I have been able to look at my life from an aerial view instead of focusing on one chapter. I can see how much growth I've had throughout the years; for that, I am grateful. There have been times that I was happy, hurting, healing, and hanging in there all at the same time. Nothing is wrong with having all of these feelings simultaneously because I am human. However, when it comes to healing, it is important to take a break from always analyzing your thoughts and behavior, because that can be exhausting, and you deserve to enjoy where you are right now.

I know there is greater for me on the other side of the pain. I could've chosen at any time to dwell on the situations that have happened and decided that I was too afraid to be hurt again, and never give love another try. But I was not built that way; I want to enjoy love. Vulnerability has allowed me to be seen for who I truly am; it has also given me the space to let go of the never-ending trap of perfectionism, too. That alone has released the pressure and given me room to make mistakes and learn from them too. If this book has accomplished anything, I hope that it will incline you to give yourself more grace, and listen to your loved ones' stories with empathy, even if you can't relate. I hope it has also given you the courage to share your own. Someone is waiting for your key to start their healing journey, too.

There have been insurmountably deep oceans that I've had to swim through, but I can see the heavens now, and in between the two is where I have had the most growth. I've been in a women's shelter, police stations, and more courtrooms than I can count because of the men that I allowed in my life, but none of those places define me as a woman. I am trusting the re-route by knowing that I have forgiven myself for the times that I have stepped away from self-love; I pray you do too.

I am a wealth of wisdom with deep experiences of love. I am no longer willing to settle for known hells while forsaking unknown heavens. I've got work to do; I am living. I have discovered that the ocean depths of my love languages could not go any deeper than the shallow pools that were created for me in most of these experiences, because they could not connect with me any deeper than they've met themselves. And now that I know better, I will choose better. Oceans and heavens are where my love has resided, and I have found both my most beautiful and tragic love stories within the two. At some point, they had to meet in the middle to birth this woman before you. Because sometimes, it is not about the ending, but more importantly about the story itself.

Made in the USA
Middletown, DE
12 September 2021